# Getting Naked

On Being Emotionally Transparent
at the Right time, the Right Place,
and with the Right Person

## PATRICK WILLIAMS

**BALBOA.**
PRESS
A DIVISION OF HAY HOUSE

Balboa Press books may be ordered through booksellers or by contacting:

Balboa Press
A Division of Hay House
1663 Liberty Drive
Bloomington, IN 47403
www.balboapress.com
1 (877) 407-4847

Because of the dynamic nature of the Internet, any web addresses or links contained in this book may have changed since publication and may no longer be valid. The views expressed in this work are solely those of the author and do not necessarily reflect the views of the publisher, and the publisher hereby disclaims any responsibility for them.

The author of this book does not dispense medical advice or prescribe the use of any technique as a form of treatment for physical, emotional, or medical problems without the advice of a physician, either directly or indirectly. The intent of the author is only to offer information of a general nature to help you in your quest for emotional and spiritual well-being. In the event you use any of the information in this book for yourself, which is your constitutional right, the author and the publisher assume no responsibility for your actions.

Any people depicted in stock imagery provided by Thinkstock are models, and such images are being used for illustrative purposes only.
Certain stock imagery © Thinkstock.

Print information available on the last page.

ISBN: 978-1-5043-5936-8 (sc)
ISBN: 978-1-5043-5935-1 (hc)
ISBN: 978-1-5043-5937-5 (e)

Library of Congress Control Number: 2016909416

Balboa Press rev. date: 07/18/2016

# Testimonials

"I've seen Patrick Williams naked (with clothes on)! What you'll read here will be honest and true and give you the courage to live the same way. This book will make a case for why you'd want to do so. Let Dr. Pat show you how covering up and hiding are doing you no favors. Let him show what you should do instead."

—Laura Berman Fortgang, author of the *Little Book on Meaning* and *Now What? 90 Days to a New Life Direction* and featured *Oprah* guest

"Yes, there are books about being authentic out there, but in today's persona-driven world where people routinely fake credentials and caring, Patrick Williams's approach is sorely needed. Patrick is authentic, optimistic, and practical in guiding us to live comfortably in our own skin and to be vulnerable and real with others. His invitation to realness is highly recommended in this disconnected, virtual world."

—Bill O'Hanlon, featured *Oprah* guest and
author of *Do One Thing Different*

"As a millennial I can say that Pat's focus on deepening our relationships through cultivating courage and living more authentically is refreshing. Reminiscent of the work of Brené Brown, *Getting Naked* is a bold, funny, and inspirational read. This book not only challenges us to think more carefully about how to build connection into our lives, but it also ultimately offers the millennial generation a road map for experiencing a more meaningful way of living and working."

—Joshua Steinfeldt, Master of Applied Positive Psychology
(MAPP) and professional certified coach

"Authenticity is one of the most admired and desired characteristics there is. Yet how often do we hold back from revealing our true self? *Getting Naked* may be just the disarming message that allows us to loosen up and learn how to be safely ourselves. People who don't reveal anything about their selves are not trusted. Those who reveal indiscriminately and often are thought to be incompetent. In this entertaining, provocative, and yet practical book, Patrick Williams helps us find the balance that can let our authentic selves flourish."

—Michael Arloski, PhD, PCC, CWP, CEO, and
founder of Real Balance Global Wellness Services,
Inc., a licensed psychologist and coach who has trained
thousands of wellness and health coaches worldwide

"*Getting Naked* is a must-read for everyone who wants to improve his or her life and relationships, be it with partners, children, parents, or friends. Coaches and therapists will find this book enlightening, refreshing, and inspirational, and so will all who work on transforming their lives."

—Cloe Madanes, author of *Relationship Breakthrough* and world-
renowned innovator and teacher of family and brief therapy

# Introduction

An expert on psychology, life, and wellness coaching, Patrick Williams believes we can never live fully or optimally if we have no places in our lives where we can be naked emotionally and spiritually. And we need to choose the right people and the right time for this self-disclosure.

He will speak about those times in his life when being naked emotionally in a safe and trusting place influenced his personal and spiritual development at various stages. He will then teach you the important and necessary requirements to find places, spaces, and times to be naked at the right time with the right people in the right way at home, work, play, and in life.

This book is not about physical nakedness. It is about being emotionally naked and transparent and spiritually vulnerable and possessing the willingness to expose one's deepest truth. I define *naked living* as the ability to be vulnerable, honest, transparent, shame-free, and unburdened.

Ideally, the master key here is to learn the power of being courageously emotionally transparent, at the *right time*, the *right place* and with the *right person*.

# Contents and Chapter Summaries

In this chapter, readers will learn from my story of various ages and stages of my journey and how I learned the power of self-revelation in the right places. This beginning will also express that life is a journey with lots of discoveries, and it will be emphasized that is true for the readers as well, no matter what life has brought them, …good, bad, or ugly

The reader will be shown how to be comfortable with who they are and how they look and feel, but underneath all that the reader learns who they are really. Exercises are shared for the reader to become more comfortable in their own skin while being vulnerable, visible, embarrassed, but also free, exhilarated, and accepting of their uniqueness.

The message in this chapter is about the importance of a playful view of the human experience. I remind the reader that no one ever lay on their deathbed wishing they had worked more…. The importance of a playful attitude and lightness of being will assist the reader about finding places and people where they can be more emotionally revealing. I will share with the reader how to lighten their load and be more playful and childlike, but not childish.

The message in this chapter is to claim the shadow as not just where we hide our deep, dark secrets, but also where we have great gifts that need to come out in the light. Furthermore, I will share stories and give examples of even finding people to share the deep dark secrets or unrevealed desires or gifts and unhook from the energy drain they can cause.

The reader will learn how transparency and honesty and emotional nakedness can find their proper place in the workplace, office, or professional group. Leadership and self-deception will be exposed as a leading cause of breakdown in companies and that can even cost profits and future success.

The message here is about modern communication via social media and how limited and even dangerous it is to self-disclose in a deep and intimate way in cyberspace. Those under 40 and especially millenials are all tweeting, texting, messaging, and even posting very personal stuff. This chapter will remind the reader that social media is NOT confidential or totally safe, and it also never goes away. I will have exercises to have real conversations with someone in real-time, not asynchronous and truncated postings to a cyber environment.

The context here is about loving relationships; spouses, partners, friends, children, family. Often the people we love and live with are the most challenging relationships we have. There are lessons to absorb by learning how and when to share soulfully and nakedly. I will share steps to open safe and powerful communication with those you love as well as learning to choose what to discuss and what to ignore and leave it be. Not all truths need to be shared…boundaries are important, and so is letting the draw bridge down for safe conversations.

Here the importance of acknowledging and accepting both the uniqueness and challenges of our body, our somatic self. And we also expose a bit about the body and aging, a time of life bringing with it an opportunity for acceptance and challenges for emotional nakedness. The metaphor of skinny dipping is one that brings up freedom and embarrassment, a paradox of our human condition.

This concluding chapter will leave the reader with the awareness that they have created their own prison from time to time in their life. I will further show how it is necessary at times to have a safe place to be, but that does not have to feel like prison. Here the reader will be given exercise and techniques to express any unshared parts of their life…. and how to experience living on purpose when it leads to emotional freedom and a more fulfilling and complete human experience

# Chapter 1

# The Power of Self-Disclosure: Stories from Your Journey

The title of this chapter comes from my experience of times in my life when emotional nakedness had good results ... eventually. This is what I want for everyone who reads this book, to either remember or to create positive outcomes from careful self-disclosure now in your life. These experiences might be memories of bumps and bruises along your journey, but they no longer need to be painful.

Just as scars are visible reminders of an injury or wound we once had, hopefully the pain that accompanied them is gone. But scars are also metaphorical and psychological reminders for those memories, experiences, and challenges that have stretched us to fully experience life as it happens, good or bad, positive or negative, or challenging or inspiring. Our life gives experiences to us. What we make of them is the key, and we don't have to do it alone. Take what life gives you, learn from it, and move forward with the help of a committed confidante or two. Someone once said, "Life is like a camera. Focus on what's important. Capture the good times. And if things don't work out, just take another shot."

One of my major beliefs for much of my life has been that personal and spiritual development is a process. You can either just let happen and be an observer, or you can be more purposeful in your personal exploration and be a participant in the unfolding or emergence of your being.

My earliest memory of learning the value of self-disclosure for the purposes of experiencing and claiming what is unique about others and myself was in my Methodist Youth Fellowship (MYF) group at age fourteen. Our youth minister would have us do some games that were geared to teach us to learn how to express ourselves and find new and unexpressed aspects of ourselves and our friends in safe and fun ways.

For example, I remember all of us being in a circle and being asked, "If you were an animal, what animal would you be?"

We were then to choose that animal and explain why we chose it, what characteristics of the animal might also be similar or desirable in our personality. Then the others in the group would comment on what they saw in me that related to that chosen animal. Or did they see me as a different animal and why?

We would then go around the group and repeat this process. It was fun and revealing without being deeply emotional. Other games and experiences like this in a safe and trusting environment, which was not confrontational, led to increased self-awareness. Within an atmosphere of curiosity and exploration, experiences like these were a major influence in my lifelong quest to be self-aware and to assist others to know themselves more fully.

As I matured into young adulthood, I was an average athlete in high school, sitting on the bench in basketball and doing well in track and field as a pole vaulter and runner. But I discovered I was accepted more at being a leader in student politics to influence a positive atmosphere for all students. I was pretty well accepted by the various cliques, groups, and races, I guess, because I cared and was curious about different human experiences while suspending judgment.

I learned the following from my early childhood as my father would frequently have foreigners stay with us for several weeks while they came to Wichita, Kansas, to learn management skills or manufacturing from the Coleman Company, where my father was the personnel director and later vice president of labor relations. Those experiences of people from India, China, Mexico, France, and others instilled in me an appreciation for different perspectives and viewpoints without being judgmental. I was just curious and fascinated.

This was tested in a very memorable way when Martin Luther King Jr. was assassinated and the black students in Wichita rioted. I was at a state track meet and hit over the head with a pipe. But my black teammates came to my aid and saved me from further damage, an act of kindness that impacted me greatly. And in the weeks following, I used my leadership and communication skills to be part of community discussion groups for quelling the racial tension and hearing from blacks, whites, and Hispanics anything they wanted to share. It was one of the best experiences of my early life. Those discussions, with an adult facilitator but with high school students having a voice, were eye-opening to me. This was an early and influential experience of being naked and vulnerable and listening to others sharing their truth and experiences in a safe environment.

As I entered college in 1968, it was a time of great transformation in society and me. I entered as a freshman wearing dress slacks and sweaters, and by 1969 I was wearing John Lennon glasses with longer hair and hippie beads and going from drinking beer to smoking pot and experimenting with hallucinogenic drugs. Yet I didn't overindulge. To me it was an experiment in living and trying new things without becoming obsessed or overly distracted. (I still made straight A's and graduated with honors.) My partying was planned to not interfere with learning. Not everyone was able to do that.

College was that place between the safety of home and the real world of working and living responsibly, which I knew was just around the corner. College in the late 1960s allowed me to experience lots of new learning, both in and out of the classroom.

I chose psychology as my path, but not to become a psychologist. I wanted to explore more about what made people tick and to learn about the good and bad along with the healthy and unhealthy of the human experience. Psychology 101 introduced me to lots of theories of human behavior, and much of those theories of child development were based on Sigmund Freud, Otto Rank, Karen Horney, and others who extolled what is called a *psychodynamic perspective.*

Freud's theories based on the belief that instincts of sex and aggression were our two main unconscious forces driving our behavior did not excite me nor resonate with my intuitive belief about being a human. And the other prevalent psychological viewpoint from behaviorism of B. F. Skinner and his followers and theories highlighting the power of operant conditioning did nothing in my view except make humans sound like unconscious robots.

Then I was fortunate enough to take a class, Psychology of Satisfaction, an experience that, to this day, was a turning point in my education and career path. It was a class about research the professor had done on an South Pacific island regarding happiness and satisfaction and which factors were influential for that to occur. In this seminar I was introduced to the theories of Carl Rogers, Abraham Maslow, Alfred Adler, and Carl Jung, four of the influencers of the Human Potential Movement and later the branch of humanistic psychology, which looked at people less mechanically and studied the farther reaches of the human experience.

That, of course, led to lots of learning opportunities in this growing Human Potential Movement and led me to attending multiple workshops at Esalen Institute in California on two occasions for a week each time. Esalen was a hub for the Human Potential Movement of the 1960s and 1970s and opened my eyes and ears to new possibilities.

These forays into self-exploration included everything from yoga and meditation to research on psychedelics, encounter groups, dance, art, music, and, of course, clothing-optional hot tubs later in the evening on this Pacific Coast paradise. Needless to say this was an eye-opening experience for me at age eighteen and nineteen, along with a transformative experience in understanding myself more in the larger scheme of things. I began to see the power of self-disclosure and experiences with being naked (figuratively and literally) in a safe and accepting environment, and I believed this was a key learning for others seeking to be more fully alive.

As I continued my studies in college, I took several classes in what at the time was called *sensitivity training*. We did things to enhance the senses: smell, touch, quiet listening, and so forth. And of course, encounter groups were the rage. I even experienced a nude encounter group as another way to lose one's masks and discover what's behind them. Again I don't share this as a way to suggest you need to get naked literally, but at those times, it was a direct link to getting naked emotionally. And it did open my eyes to the varieties of the human experience and find ways to feel free to take off our protective armor.

Some of these experiences were not so good, as a motto of the time was "Let it all hang out" or "Tell it like it is." Sometimes these groups were an excuse for people to be mean and attacking, but I survived. And there were many other times when tender and deep emotional sharing took place that engendered even more my desire for exploring the human experience as fully as possible.

Surviving and thriving in the 1970s experience—and yes, there were many lessons—then took me to the real world for a year of working for Hallmark Cards Crown Center Project in Kansas City. I could not stand it with the corporate culture, office cubicle, and management hierarchy, and so off I went to get a master's degree in humanistic psychology at University of West Georgia in Carrollton, Georgia, a town of twelve thousand mostly Southern Baptists and rural folks who had a tolerant relationship with the college psychology students who were studying "weird things" in their estimation.

And yet I met many locals at antique fairs and country jamborees and immersed myself in the Southerner experience for the two years I was in Georgia. My wife, on the other hand, did not enjoy moving from her home of Leawood and Overland Park, Kansas, saying she went across several states she'd never been in before.

Looking back, I know she felt out of place and disconnected, even though family visited and we had fun. She was not fond of living in Georgia. More than twenty years later when we would get divorced, I learned this was actually the beginning for her of feeling lonely and weary of my willingness to be such a risk taker and explorer.

We had a great twenty-one years together, but the divorce brought a new reckoning for me with what I was hiding at the time. The challenges with my two teenage daughters did cause some painful experiences then. Happily, all is well now, more than twenty years into

relationship with my new wife and my new life. I cherish the
ity of my daughters, grandkids, my stepson, and step-grandkids,
even have an amicable relationship with my former wife.

The humanistic psychology program at University of West Georgia
was a continuation of exploring human potential in multiple ways from
Eastern philosophy, Jungian psychology, parapsychology, and other
studies in consciousness. And luminaries in the field and many visiting
scholars of renown taught me. It was a hotbed of humanistic psychology.

A transformational experience that took place and impacted my
world ever since was my meeting Sidney Jourard, a famous Canadian
psychologist, at a fish fry at a professor's house. He had come to guest
lecture and was famous for his theories on the importance of self-
disclosure expressed in his book, *The Transparent Self.*

He was staying in town for a while, and I handed him my copy of
the book for his signature, which he gladly wrote. Then I stated how
much I liked it and said I wanted to write a book someday.

He said, "Give me the book again." And then he wrote, "Pat, if you
never write your book, you have no one to blame but yourself." And
then he signed his name, Sid.

In those few minutes, he had gone from Dr. Jourard to Sid and left
me a personal message that impacted me then and now.

But the real story is this: the next day, my professor shared the
sad news that, while Sidney was working on his car outside his home
in Tallahassee, Florida, the jack collapsed. The car fell on Sidney,
killing him!

You can imagine how his message to me revolved in my brain
for years until I published my first book in 1980, *Transpersonal
Psychology and the Evolution of Consciousness*, which was designed for
an introductory course on transpersonal psychology. I sold thousands
of copies over a few years to colleges, and then it became outdated and
is now out of print today.

In 2002 I co-authored my first professionally published book with
Norton Books, *Therapist as Life Coach: Transforming your Practice*,
which I dedicated to Sidney Jourard. And I have co-authored six
other books, which all sold well, but they are all professional books.

This book, *Getting Naked*, however, is the book Sidney Jourard was challenging me to write.

A choice, which confronts each of us at every moment, is this: Will we allow others to know us as we now are, or shall we seek instead to remain an enigma, wishing to be seen as something we are not? Throughout history, humans seem to have chosen the road of concealment rather than "openness." Professor Jourard maintained that this strategy all too often results in sickness, misunderstanding, and alienation of self.

My favorite poem, "The Road Not Taken" by Robert Frost, has been a symbolic view of how I have always cherished the less chosen path.

> Two roads diverged in a wood, and I—
> I took the one less traveled by,
> And that has made all the difference.

In *The Transparent Self*, Sidney Jourard's premise is that self-concealment can lead to "sickness, misunderstanding, and alienation from self." He argues that "man can attain health and fullest personal development only insofar as he gains courage to be himself with others and only when he finds goals that have meaning for him, goals which include the reshaping of society so that it is fit for all to live and grow in."[1]

His idea of a fully functioning human being was someone who had at least one person in his or her life with whom he or she could talk about anything. Without that, he contended our psychological health would suffer, and our efforts to grow would be held back.

My friend and colleague Michael Arloski, a renowned wellness coach and author, writes about Jourard and his studies of self-disclosure. In his 1968 book, *Disclosing Man to Himself*, he shared work he had done on self-disclosure in counseling groups.

---

[1]   Sidney Jourard, *The Transparent Self* (D. Van Norstand Company, Inc., 1964).

**Trust, Self-disclosure and Groups:**

> Counseling group members were identified as having disclosed about themselves in one of three ways over the course of the group experience: 1) self-disclosed very little, 2) self-disclosed a lot and early in the group, or 3) self-disclosed gradually over the course of the group. The level of trust that the group members felt towards each other was then measured. Surprisingly the group trusted the least was not group number one, but rather group number two. Those who shared too much about themselves too fast were trusted the least. The gradual self-disclosers were trusted the most. This lines up with the personal experience most of us have with self-disclosure in our daily lives. People who reveal deeply and rapidly often repel us. **This is because** self-disclosure is reciprocal. **The expectation is for you to match the self-disclosure leve**l of the other person."[2]

So if you are not a revealer and are around someone who shares to the extreme, you will likely be uncomfortable. Find those who speak and listen with your rhythm, which provides safety and comfort for honest and meaningful conversation.

My encounter with Professor Jourard was a marvelous shared experience of respect and encouragement by one of psychotherapy's shining lights. I learned so much from him in his books, and my short meeting with him in person sealed the deal.

*Getting Naked* is about learning how to be open about your authentic self with the rest of the world, at least those you trust. It is about how being secretive about yourself can lead to physical, mental, and emotional sickness. Can we actually try to live healthier by being honest with our fellow humans about who and how we are?

---

[2]  http://realbalancewellness.wordpress.com/2012/03/02/self-disclosure-in-coaching-when-sharing-helps-and-hinders

Get real. Be authentic. Be courageous. Make contact and empathize. Trust and disclose yourself, and invite others to do the same.

I share all this history to say how that transformational moment came from me sheepishly sharing at a moment of feeling naked at age twenty-five to a prominent author and psychologist that I wanted to write a book. And when he challenged me with a wink and his statement, I knew someday I would.

When you are honest with another and share what you have kept hidden or at least well disguised, it invokes what I call the *unexpected turn*. Every conversation presents the opportunity for two experiences. It is both common and predictable with no surprises and little revelatory information, or it takes an unexpected turn. Once you are surprisingly honest with a trusted friend or colleague (or they with you), it usually leads to a more heartfelt and personally connected conversation.

Granted, many conversations are just meant to be mundane and as expected, but how would it be if you sought out opportunities for self-disclosure? If you asked someone, "What are your passions or big desires? Tell me something exciting in your life" instead of our usual greeting of "How ya doing?" that would lead to more truthful and useful dialogue.

**Exercise: Who in your life—living or dead—has inspired you? Does this person know that he or she had that impact? If this individual is still alive, tell him or her!**

Following my master's degree, I then enrolled at University of Northern Colorado's School of Educational Change and Development, which at the time allowed me to choose a doctoral committee, design a degree program, and take courses from any department or off campus if it met the academic requirements for the doctor of education. I developed my program curricula in transpersonal psychology and counseling, emphasizing courses in states of consciousness, somatic psychology, psychobiology, and Eastern philosophy and practices such as psychosynthesis, psychodrama techniques, meditation, biofeedback, and more, anything that synthesized body, brain, and being.

Again I was seeking to know my self (everyday awareness) and my self (higher consciousness), the higher self, the being that is my experience and the experience that is my being. My journey was to explore what is greater than our self or our everyday awareness, that is, what pulls us forward into meaning, purpose, and connection to all living things. As Teilhard de Chardin famously said, "We are not human beings having a spiritual experience. We are spiritual beings having a human experience."

One of my experiences of naked living happened at age twenty-seven while I was on a nineteen-day Outward Bound expedition with twenty-four other adults in Canyonlands National Park in Utah. We were split up in three patrols of eight each and taught to read topographical maps, find safe drinking water, rappel down canyon walls, and rock climb as well.

On one particular day, we were being taught basic rock climbing while connected by rope to an instructor above us on the sheer wall we were to climb. We were belayed below to another guide holding the climbing rope. I loved the feeling of rappelling and felt safe with the ropes and braking systems, but rock climbing up while looking for footholds and handholds was a bit more frightening. Even though being belayed to an instructor above, knowing I could not fall far if I did lose my grip, the view of the expanse and the steepness of the climb was visually scary. At the time of my climb, I reached a place on the wall where I was not feeling secure and unsure I could reach the next good place to grab with my hand. My foot was shaking up and down, and my whole body felt tight.

I looked down at my instructor, who said, "You're feeling afraid. That's okay. Go ahead and be present with your fear. And when you are ready, then reach up for the next hold."

I remember that moment to this day, of feeling so vulnerable, scared, and embarrassed.

But then he said, "We all feel fear. Acknowledge and then move."

That has been a guide to me all my life. After all I was roped on to guides and really could not have been hurt. I was just feeling naked on the wall and embarrassed that I was not braver. "Feel the fear, and move on" has been a motto for my life ever since. Or it's similar to the famous British WWII slogan, "Keep calm and carry on."

Brené Brown's work on vulnerability and the concept of wholeheartedness is wonderful research and life lessons for being more courageous. We can be deliberate and careful in revealing or discovering the person we really are while also establishing strong boundaries and being very deliberate about when and with whom to share. Her books *The Gifts of Imperfection* and *Daring Greatly* are wonderful titles and worth reading on your journey to living optimally and fully. She says in *The Gifts of Imperfection*,

> Owning our story can be hard but not nearly as difficult as spending our lives running from it. Embracing our vulnerabilities is risky but not nearly as dangerous as giving up on love, belonging, and joy—the experiences that make us the most vulnerable. Only when we are brave enough to explore the darkness will we discover the infinite power of our light.[3]

My journey continued after college and through many life events—becoming a psychologist, having two daughters, engaging in family life, growing my business, and becoming involved in local politics and community leadership.

A big schism occurred in what felt like my perfect life and family when my wife suddenly announced she wanted a divorce and left with her new lover, leaving my daughters and me with tears and fears on our front porch. My daughters were sixteen and fourteen, and we all were left with total shock and confusion, as none of us had seen that coming.

The weeks and months that followed were a blur. I still worked. They still went to school and did not want to see their mother for many weeks. I was able to share my grief and anger with colleagues at my psychology practice, but the pain I saw in my daughters' faces was

---

[3]    Brené Brown, *The Gifts of Imperfection* (Center City, Minn.: Hazelden, 2010).

devastating. I did not know what to do. Looking back now, there were lots of mistakes, ones you don't realize until you are way down the road. There is no manual for divorce adjustment for kids.

Fast-forward two years, after a little dating, I met a woman who would later become my wife, and although the girls liked her, they did not really like me with someone else. However, two months after I met her, she had to go back to Florida where her mother was diagnosed with pancreatic cancer and had six months or less to live.

So we had a long-distance relationship for many months. But the communication via phone calls and long letters and cards, as there was no Internet for me and no cell phones either, actually helped our relationship as we both shared truths in our long calls and letters, a necessary ingredient for any relationship.

My memory of that time is a blur really. I know we all struggled. Even my new girlfriend and I struggled in our new relationship, as we were both recently divorced for two years or so. We kept dating. My oldest started college, and my youngest was living with her mother now and finishing high school. There were many challenges with their and my behavior and the emptiness we were all three looking to heal. I admittedly began drinking way too much, and that created some anger and distancing (rightfully so) with my daughters and my love. It was like I was doing the exact thing I knew would be damaging, but I felt helpless and alone a lot.

Things seem to get better, and by the end of 1996, my girlfriend and I decided to move to Florida to start over. I figured the girls were starting their adult lives, as they were now twenty and eighteen. Truthfully I don't even remember all that period. My youngest moved to Oregon, where her mother and new husband-to-be were moving for his job. My oldest was in college, living with other students.

I had also created a somewhat superficial and yet acceptable relationship with the two sons of my new love. We all even celebrated Thanksgiving together with my daughters and the ex-husband of my new love and her sons. Today it is actually a story they would all talk about with a little laughter and funny stories about their experiences.

Yes, we are still together, and my oldest daughter works for my new wife's son in Colorado. My youngest daughter lives with roommates in Oregon and seems happy. And with a great group of friends, she's doing what she loves with an adventurous and loving spirit. And we all get together a few times a year for vacations or visits.

The move to Florida was hurtful to all of us. It caused a lot of painful conversations and then some breakthroughs as well as time went on. We ended up back in Colorado in 2000, and all relationships and my business began to really improve. My coaching business was booming, and I was really happy not to be a clinical psychologist anymore. In 2006 we again moved back to Florida, thinking we would also keep a house or condo in Colorado, but the economic downturn caused us to sell all properties and just stay in Florida. As it has turned out, things are great for my wife and me, and my relationship with my daughters is very good. Focusing on being wholehearted, as Brené Brown says, also leads to extraordinary learning. We can be imperfect, but also brave, loving, and worthy of belonging and connecting.

Of course my daughters don't share everything with me, but we do have meaningful father-daughter conversations, and I praise them for who they have become without talking about what they went through.

In my own life experience and work, I have seen many examples of people become happier, and their relationships became more fulfilling once they truly learned to be real. One notable experience comes to mind from my early career as a psychologist. I had completed my doctorate but was interning at the college counseling center to benefit from the supervision of the center's director. I had a few clients in the summer session, usually young students stressed by their new college life away from home or the hurt of breaking up with a significant other.

My counseling seemed helpful and showed me that I was a good listener and able to normalize their experiences. Through client-centered counseling, I could assist them in gaining insight, new behaviors, and a transformed mind-set that helped them feel more empowered and ready to get back into life.

## An Early Counseling Experience as a Young Therapist

One day I got a call from a young woman who said her friend had told her I was a good counselor. She wondered if I could meet her. I said of course, so we set up an appointment. When she arrived for her appointment, I asked what brought her in.

She said, "I'll show you."

She proceeded to take off her shoes and socks and then pointed to her feet. They were covered with cut marks.

She looked at me with a blank stare and said, "I cut my feet and then pour muriatic acid on them."

Later in my career, I learned that this was an effective way to feel pain and then immediate numbness. This is often the goal for someone with an abusive history and who feels lost, alone, disconnected, or invisible.

Inside, my stomach turned, and my mind was in shock, but apparently I did not show that on the outside. While showing only a calm, caring demeanor, I asked, "And what causes you to do that?"

She asked, "Why are you not horrified at this stupid and repulsive behavior?"

I asked, "Why should I be?"

She proceeded to tell me that it seemed to be a way of numbing her feelings of loss in her life. Eventually she shared with me about being beaten often as a child in an alcoholic family. Later on in my career, I would see many cutters in my office and usually uncovered their stories of sexual abuse as young girls.

A supervision session with my director followed my experience in this first session with her. I felt I had to be naked now. *Had I done the right thing? Said the right words? What was she going to do next? If she came back, what would be my protocol for treatment?* My supervisor asked me how I felt about my session. And I said I guess it went okay. I had listened and did not react with disgust or shock to my client. My neutral response seemed to give the girl a safe place to be vulnerable and trusting with me, whom she had just met.

My supervisor told me I had done very well, and we talked about details of the case and ways to proceed. I had over twelve sessions with her that ultimately turned out very well. She changed her destructive behaviors, became more involved in activities, met some new friends, and seemed to be on a path of healing. Her revelation to me and my support assisted her in unloading a heavy burden. She no longer needed to instigate self-abuse in order to feel numb. My therapeutic process with her became a huge stepping-stone on my own journey of becoming real.

Much more has happened of course in my journey, both wonderful and hurtful, but these events are my story of how I came to value and honor self-disclosure based upon ages and stages in my life. The early years, the adolescent period, young adulthood, college, marriage, parenthood, career path, and aging are part of our stretch marks, or bumps and bruises.

We all are a compilation of our experiences, memories, and perception of those. What we learn from them is the key. Chosen change—or unchosen change—all eventually has to be accepted and digested, and then life continues. These times are when you need someone to be emotionally naked with, as I have many times, and those lessons are what this book is about for you.

What key points of your life have affected your way of living and what you share or don't? How could that change if you found the place and person to share what you have not shared, to say what you have not said, and to dream out loud with a caring listener?

Responses to events are mediated. In other words, once an event takes place, our responses—our behaviors—are shaped by

- our interpretation of the event, a consequence of our beliefs, attitudes, and assumptions, and
- the feelings generated by those beliefs, attitudes, and assumptions.

Those beliefs, attitudes, and assumptions are the preexisting lenses we wear and look through, which determine or at least color our observation and interpretation of events.

Now read on and discover ways and means to be naked emotionally when it is safe and secure, and you will find yourself feeling more whole and open in the right times, places, and circumstances and with the right people. And you will become more Real, as the next chapter illuminates.

# Chapter 2

# Becoming Real: The Velveteen Rabbit Principle

"History is not just facts and events. History is also a pain in the heart and we repeat history until we are able to make another's pain in the heart our own."

—Sue Monk Kidd, *The Invention of Wings*

To break free of the patterns that bind us, we need to tear down the iron curtain of our public selves. Becoming real is inextricably intertwined with another fully seeing us. Instead of hiding from our pain, we need to befriend and tend it. We do that by feeling the pain, naming it, and, surprisingly, sharing our pain with another. The ability to become clearer about who you are and accurate about what you bring to life is what I call *naked truth*.

I share several stories later in this book, but for now, let this one illustrate what I mean. It was around the holiday season when a coaching client who had worked with me for many months seemed unusually distracted and even sad. I told her I had not seen that before in our time together, and I asked if there were something she wanted to share about her current state of emotions and thoughts.

She paused, got tearful, and then said, "I have never told anyone this, but at age eighteen, long before I was married, I chose to have an abortion from a pregnancy I did not want. I was not ready for that responsibility. I felt guilty and ashamed. Today I wonder, especially in this season, who that child might have been. In all the debate today about abortion being the woman's decision, I still feel guilty about choosing to end the future life of a fetus, and that often leaves me feeling sad and empty."

I paused in reverent silence and gave my client the space to continue.

She then said after a long, tearful silence, "You know, even though it still hurts, it feels better finally sharing that. I feel like a weight was just taken from my insides, and I can now breathe differently. Thank you."

The point here is not to judge what my client had done but to see the value in her being able to reveal her secret so it could no longer steal parts of who she was. Her humanness is not different in essence than that of anyone else. We all have faced hardship and have had to make difficult decisions, but my client's beingness was unique to her. And she reclaimed a big part of that by sharing her truth honestly with me.

We are, in essence, relationship beings. If you live your life never revealing things that you have kept hidden, your authentic self will always be hidden as well. You will be loved by some and befriended by others, but something crucial will be missing. You will feel a hole somewhere inside of you, and that hole will keep you from feeling whole. In addition, if there are dreams or aspirations that you have given up on or stuffed away, you are likely to feel unfulfilled in your calling. Likewise, if there are stories of abuse, hurt, loss, grief, shame, or guilt related to life experiences that you have also buried, you will have to live with the burden of keeping them hidden and protected.

The point is not to share these parts of yourself with everyone or just anyone. It is to find a trusted listener who will keep your stories sacred and personal. Naked living asks you to find that committed and trusted other and simply share the stories from your shadowy storage space and then reclaim the energy that is attached to keeping them in hiding.

The witness is key. You can be emotionally naked by yourself, and there is value to that experience, yet it can only take you so far. Being emotionally naked during a relational experience with a trusted other has the power to evoke even deeper revelations. It must be a relational experience with a trusted other to be transformative.

As one of my mentors, Sidney Jourard, put so articulately,

> "Disclosure is so important (because) without it we really cannot know ourselves. Or to put it another way, we learn to deceive ourselves while we are trying to deceive others. For example, if I never express my sorrow, my love, my joy, I'll smother those feelings in myself until I almost forget they were once part of me." (Notes from his lecture in 1975, University of West Georgia)

When you keep some stories hidden in the shadow of your soul, that is what I call surviving, not thriving.

As previously cited, and worth repeating here, in The *Transparent Self*, Sidney Jourard's presents the premise that self-concealment can lead to "sickness, misunderstanding, and alienation from self." He argues "man can attain health and fullest personal development only insofar as he gains courage to be himself with others." Jourard's idea of a fully functioning human being was someone who had at least one person in his or her life with whom he or she could talk about anything. Without that, he contended our psychological health would suffer, and our efforts to grow would be held back.

Here's what some of my clients report about their experience of being emotionally naked and how it relates to others.

## Naked in Their Own Words

o   "Nakedness is to be bare and show your authentic self. To me, naked is to allow your self to be real and vulnerable. It is to be vivid, tender, vulnerable, and helpless."

- ○ "To be emotionally naked to me is feeling strong and free with who I am, and if someone doesn't like it, then they don't like me. Oh, well. I can only be who I am."
- ○ "Naked can feel terrifying, particularly if you work very hard to hide things from people, such as secrets that you fear will not be liked and accepted."
- ○ "Letting go of 'creating' how I look on the outside. There is no preparation of emotional nakedness. It is 'being' without reservation or censorship."
- ○ "It's terrifying that others could see your faults. But when you are able to learn the lesson and move past it, you feel stronger."

Whether implicit or explicit, each of these definitions reveals how emotional nakedness occurs relative to the other. Their quotes imply that being naked lets them reframe their experience of vulnerability into one of empowerment.

## What It Means to Be Real

In *The Velveteen Rabbit* by Margery Williams, "real" is what happens when you become who you truly are, not some falsely created, superficial, glossy, pretentious image. You are loved for all you have withstood, every mishap, and every vigorous snuggle session. In the story, the little boy has forgotten an old favorite toy, the Velveteen Rabbit, a stuffed bunny with no electric parts, motors, technology, and glitz.

Abandoned after the excitement of Christmas and stored with the older toys, the Velveteen Rabbit is comforted by the wise, old Skin Horse who predicts that the boy will once again love him. The horse is correct: the Velveteen Rabbit is later chosen to comfort the boy through a terrible illness. The boy and Velveteen Rabbit's mutual enjoyment in each other transforms the toy into what the Skin Horse calls real.

> "What is REAL?" asked the Rabbit one day, when they were lying side by side near the nursery fender, before

Nana came to tidy the room. "Does it mean having things that buzz inside you and a stick-out handle?"

"Real isn't how you are made," said the Skin Horse. "It's a thing that happens to you. When a child loves you for a long, long time not just to play with, but REALLY loves you, then you become Real."

"Does it hurt?"

"Sometimes," said the Skin Horse, for he was always truthful. "When you are Real you don't mind being hurt."

"Does it happen all at once," he asked, "or bit by bit?"

"It doesn't happen all at once," said the Skin Horse. "You become. It takes a long time. That's why it doesn't happen to people who break easily, or have sharp edges, or who have to be carefully kept. Generally, by the time you are Real, most of your hair has been loved off, and your eyes drop out and you get loose in the joints, and very shabby. But those things don't matter at all, because once you are real you can't be ugly, except to people who don't understand."[4]

The first time I read this book so many years ago as a young father, its message struck me. The idea of realness resonated through my core. It was a metaphor for being in relationships, taking risks, and accepting hurts. It nailed the tension between the superficial beauty that so many of us get obsessed with and the real, inner loveliness we possess when we are attuned to our realness.

In a life well lived, people will show the scars, age spots, warts, and wrinkles, but they only make individuals more lovable. For this

---

[4]  Margery Williams, *The Velveteen Rabbit* (George H. Doran Company, 1922).

transformative acceptance to occur, however, we need to feel comfortable in our own skin.

The Velveteen Rabbit's message is not just a bromide regarding aging. It goes beyond appearance to delve into the essence of our humanity, finding peace in our embodied form despite its vulnerability and impermanence. In my own life experience and work, I have seen many examples of people becoming happier and their relationships more fulfilling once they learned to be truly real. One notable experience comes to mind from my career as a therapist.

Vikki, a pseudonym, had come to me for help with her severe depression and marital strife. For over four years, we worked on her low self-esteem, lack of intimacy, perceived helplessness, and parenting frustrations. Her coping strategy was dissociative behavior consisting mainly of cutting her arms and legs with a sharp knife. The cutting was not intended to cause massive bleeding. The goal was sharp pain, followed by numbing, which was my client's way of making herself temporarily unreal.

Cutting is fairly typical behavior among those who were molested, raped, or abused in childhood. The cutting causes brief stinging pain; a release of endorphins follows. The next stage is a period of physical and emotional numbness, an escape from reality, but only a temporary one. The cutting hangover is a pervasive sense of shame and helplessness. These deeply uncomfortable feelings spur a person to seek further numbing and escape, and so the unhealthy cycle continues.

Over time, with the help of hypnosis, journaling exercises, and disclosure, Vikki began to realize that her reenactment of her primary wounding was a legitimate expression of despair. Instead of continuing to feel shame about these behaviors, she could finally understand and claim them. The process of confiding in me and receiving unconditional positive regard from me as she shared her truth allowed her to feel normal. Becoming real is similar to what therapists refer to as *normalization*, reframing a client's problem situation as human and worthy of acceptance.

Coming out of the cutting closet was a huge relief for my client. Her ability to share with me transformed the pathology in her struggle into an opportunity for her to experience my empathy, to be understood nonjudgmentally by someone else, which in turn gave her permission to understand herself with that same lack of judgment. She began to reclaim her adult life.

I suggested she write letters to her younger self, thanking the young self for surviving and introducing her adult self to the child self. My client was a beautifully expressive writer. She allowed me to read some of her prose and poetry expressing her innermost thoughts and feelings. She eventually integrated her child self into her current life by reassuring her younger self that it was now safe to be present. She promised to love, protect, and recognize her fragile inner child. We terminated therapy successfully, and she carried on with her life.

When I closed my therapy practice a few years later and opened my new professional coaching business, she read about me and asked to see me. I told her I no longer did therapy, and she told me she did not want therapy. She wanted coaching. After thoroughly discussing the new boundaries and ethics of seeing me as a coach (specifically stating that any therapy would be done with someone else) and other goals for coaching, I agreed to work with her.

As it turned out, her goal was to publish a book of her poetry or to get some of her poems published. Many of the poems were about her abuse, directly or metaphorically, but they also had an undercurrent of redemption and empowerment. I told her truthfully that I found them quite moving. Her goal was to get at least one poem published. She thought that would prove that her story could be meaningful to others who had suffered childhood trauma. She was willing to get emotionally naked not just in my presence but also in front of her potential readers.

I gave her an assignment of getting ten rejection letters in the next few weeks, which she thought was a weird request. I explained that getting rejections was par for the course and in fact made becoming published more of a reality. Ultimately an academic journal on women's issues agreed to publish some of her poetry. She also co-authored a little book of poems that sold locally in bookstores.

From self-loathing she had embarked on a journey of self-discovery and compassion. Her willingness to be real with herself and the world became literally the stuff of poetry. A core aspect of Vikki's transition from numb to naked was her ability to let go of blame of herself and her abuser. While owning our story is important, it's equally important to not get too hung up on it. Blame keeps us in the smallness of our stories. It holds us to the sidelines of life, giving us an ever-ready excuse of why we can't be a contender. Speaking our story out loud frees us from being benched in victimhood. Dialogue expands the playing field, giving us the power to get back into the game.

And so it went with my client. Once Vikki was able to dialogue with me about her hidden parts, these hidden parts became real and powerful and could evolve into poetry. She was back on the playing field of life, participating and engaging. Becoming real is an interdependent process whose reward is, paradoxically, true independence. Once we speak our truth and are listened to with loving ears, that acceptance allows us to take responsibility for our story. As we are accepted, so we become able to accept ourselves. Being honest about yourself may seem to be difficult at first, but it gets easier with practice and maturity

Returning to the story of *The Velveteen Rabbit*, let's not forget the other key character, the Skin Horse, who plays the role of the accepting other. We could almost say that the Skin Horse plays the role of the Velveteen Rabbit's life coach! Once the Velveteen Rabbit confides in him and shares his despair, the Skin Horse is kind, empathetic, sensitive, and always truthful. He models emotional nakedness and demonstrates his trustworthiness as a confidante. He normalizes the Velveteen Rabbit's flaws and makes him see they are nothing to be ashamed of. In fact they are badges of honor.

> "I suppose you are Real?" said the Rabbit. And then he wished he had not said it, for he thought the Skin Horse might be sensitive. But the Skin Horse only smiled. "The boy's uncle made me Real," he said. "That was a great many years ago; but once you become Real, you can't become unreal again. It lasts for always."[5]

---

[5]  Ibid.

The Velveteen Rabbit's empowerment was twofold. He could now experience real relationships with others, and he could also enjoy the newfound autonomy that realness bestows. If the Skin Horse weren't such a good listener, the Velveteen Rabbit would never have discovered the truth he needed in order to become real himself. The sharing conversation was transformational for the Velveteen Rabbit.

We must, I believe, have a conversation about what we are thinking inside to be heard on the outside, but only with a great and committed listener. The magic of revealing ourselves to a trusted other allows us to reclaim energy that has been keeping the cellar door locked.

During my career as a coach, I created an exercise called the "personal treasure hunt." It's an exercise in reframing your perspective, which can resonate deeply. Reframing is a tool for putting an experience in a new frame, to shift your perspective and get a new point of view. I strongly request that you carve out some quality time for this exercise and see it through to its completion.

## Exercise: Personal Treasure Hunt

For this exercise you will need a piece of paper, a pen, and about twenty minutes of solitude in a comfortable, quiet space.

## Part One

Draw a line down the middle of a piece of paper, and then invite an attitude of quiet reflection. On the left side, write the names of people you have admired, living or dead. Then on the right side, list your reasons for why you admire each person. What qualities are you drawn to? Think about special talents, values, strengths, acts of kindness, and ways in which these have become visible in his or her life choices.

Once you have completed this list, fold the paper along the centerline so only the qualities on the right can be seen. Now take a good, long look and read the traits or qualities out loud, pausing to reflect on the words. Do this carefully because the traits you have listed here about others are also a part of you. Some may be aspects or traits you have quietly tried to develop in your life; others may be aspects of you that are hiding in your shadow. Either way let this exercise be a profound moment of recognition. You have these traits, whether they are expressed right now or not.

Now that you know the traits you value, do you want to continue living as a person you don't admire, or are there opportunities for you to change how you show up in your life?

**Part Two**

Now that you have completed the first task, try this follow-up exercise. Think of a handful of people whom you know you can trust to be honest, those who know you now as well as people who knew you way back when, such as high school chums. Ask them what they would say are the traits or attributes they see in you that are similar to traits in themselves that they like. Acknowledge to them that this may seem like an odd exercise, but let them know you are doing an experiment.

The outcomes you will gain are some surprising revelations of gifts you have that you were not aware of or unique ways you have impacted friends or family. By the completion of this exercise, you will be filled up with treasures that may have you feeling humility and joy.

If you are really brave and willing to be naked, ask your spouse or long-time partner what made you attractive back when you first met. Then do the same for your spouse or partner. You may either do this as a reflective conversation, or write down your answers and share later. Either way, you are mining gold and gems that have been hidden under the dust in your life.

Take it all in, and fill your metaphorical shoulder bag with these treasures. Put them in a safe place. They will help you become ever more real to yourself. On days when you are feeling a little blue or disconnected, admire your gems. They are always a part of who you are, and they will guide you on whatever path you are walking.

## Celebrating Imperfection

When my daughters were youngsters, they loved to make and decorate cookies. Just for fun, we sometimes experimented with adding cinnamon, peanut butter, or candy. The cookies we made together were different shapes, sizes, and even textures. Some were sugar cookies; others were chocolate chip. A few were oatmeal. To enjoy them fully, we had to let go of any expectation of what a cookie was supposed to look like. I talked to them about how store-bought cookies all looked the same—neat, sterile, and boring. We started enjoying the different shapes, sizes, and creative decorations. After all, who was going to eat them? Just us. (We did share some.) The misshapen cookies expressed the messy deliciousness of our own humanity.

We often think we are not perfect. In fact, perfect does not exist. We are all unique and one of a kind with a calling or life purpose for being on this planet. Imperfections, as we call them, are just uniqueness. You are not in a baking contest, per se. You are living your life, and judgment from others is only their point of view, neither right nor wrong.

What do you think about you? Who are you in essence? Can you love yourself and then change what you choose to change for you? Because you want to; not because others say you should. Once you accept that imperfections make us homemade, you can begin to embrace the meaning of real.

To be real, you have to risk not meeting other people's expectations, and you have to be willing to meet the parts of yourself you have been trying to deny. Our flaws are merely the shadow aspect of our potential. They long to be held, cherished, nurtured, and brought into the light. Once we can honor our flaws and remain open to our potential, we can move toward our dreams, just as Vikki was able to turn shame into poetry. And once you live your life that way, you inspire others to do the same. Once you become real, you encourage others to live life more on the edge, to take chances, to not be shamed, and to exemplify a sense of wonder, curiosity, and openness rather than cynicism, fear, and loneliness.

## A Lawyer's Transformation

I had another client whose life changed radically once she was willing to get real with me as we worked together to take a closer look at her motives. I specialized in coaching attorneys for several years as part of a business development course they took. My goal was to help each lawyer implement new strategies to work more efficiently, cultivate his or her ideal client base, and meet more of his or her personal goals.

A few months into the coaching, I sensed a lack of motivation on one of my client's part. I asked about it. I knew she was successful, made great money, and even liked many of her clients. Valerie was a contract lawyer and did estate planning. I asked her to tell me how and why she became an attorney. What did she like about the law?

Her response was to pause for several seconds. Then she said, "I never really wanted to be a lawyer. My dad wanted me to and said I could segue into his successful practice."

As it turned out, law was never her dream. It was her father's.

"What was your dream?" I asked.

"I always wanted to be a teacher, but my father said that career was not good enough for me."

"So you've been living someone else's dream," I said, exposing the truth for her.

Valerie wanted to teach. She found herself happiest when leading seminars on estate planning or teaching at women's shelters and other community organizations. I explored what her response would be if a teaching opportunity came up. She said she had never given it much thought. I then coached her to look for opportunities at local colleges, especially law schools, where she would have the necessary expertise.

Several months later, after expressing her interest in a teaching position, a well-known law school in her state asked her to apply. Anticipating an imminent job offer, I then coached her on how to have a truthful conversation with her parents.

Even though she anticipated the conversation with dread, after she had shared her part, her father told her that he was proud of her for being so truthful. He had only assumed she wanted to be a lawyer like him because she seemed to like it. She cried as she related the conversation, and I told her how much it touched me as well.

She ended up closing her law practice after a few months and taking the job. She adjusted her lifestyle to match her lower salary and reported she was happier than she had been in years. Wow! She was dating a wonderful man and doing what she loved while still honoring her field of expertise.

In what ways do you hide from your own truth? In what ways does your desire to be good get in the way of your own happiness? Your shadow, your unconscious potential, contains many valuable insights that need to be plumbed. You can do this by journaling, reflecting, and/or working with a coach. Coaches ask what we in the trade refer to as powerful questions, those that evoke new thinking, visions, and possibilities. Here are some examples of powerful questions:

- If money were no issue, what would you be doing?
- What assumptions are you making, and what are the facts?
- How would you like things to be different a year from now?
- What are you missing or avoiding?
- What dreams have you given up on?

To become real is to risk baring your truth to someone. Take the leap of nakedness. You will discover, many masters have taught, the part of us that wants to *become* is fearless. When we let go of needing it to look a certain way, the imperfect becomes our paradise.

## Finding Your Legs

Our wounds can mask our greatest gifts. Once we can reframe our wounds into an opportunity for growth, we tap into a fierce resilience we didn't even know we had. Oftentimes though, we keep our wounds hidden in our shadow self, alongside our secrets, thinking this will somehow keep us safe. The shadow serves as some dark place where we can unconsciously keep all the bad parts of ourselves that we don't want to acknowledge and don't want others to encounter. Yet in our shadow lies not only our dark side but also our unrealized strengths and creativity.

When we shine light on the wounds and the secrets in our shadow self, we invite a more authentic way of living. I will say more about this in chapter 4, but let me just say here that wholeness comes from the ability to open the vault on occasion and share our dreams and aspirations or hurts and scars with another so they don't suck the life force out of you like a psychic vampire.

One way of recognizing our shadow is to pay attention to what strongly attracts or repels us in others. What kind of person are you attracted to? What kind of person really repels you or do you choose to avoid? What is a part of yourself that you wish would just go away?

Many times I have heard my clients say something like, "I have this problem or old wound, and I would like to resolve it or make it go away." I have found what we want so much to go away sticks to us like Velcro. Instead of pushing it away, by acknowledging it first for yourself and then with another, you can ironically find the resolution you seek.

Once we dare to dream, we make way for our own potential to tunnel through. We find a way to give our truth legs to walk the world with. When we engage in naked conversation, we create a sacred space for what we want to be different in our life now and in the future to emerge.

Sometimes dwelling for too long on our negatively charged memories and beliefs doesn't serve us. As a coach, I have discovered, while wounds can illuminate, they can also hold us back. The trick is to find the closeness of the wound to the gift. It can be disguised as the positive shadow, which gets projected on to others as admiration or envy. A good way to channel that envy is to focus on what's alive in you now. Your current desires, as opposed to your past fears, are the most important influence on the blueprint you can design for your future.

## Dancing in the Shadows

I had a client whose progress illustrates how following the trail of envy can lead you to your deepest longing. After several years of coaching, I wrote some articles on retirement coaching, what I called *legacy coaching*. I targeted people who had either retired or were looking to shift their work to philanthropy or professional volunteering and thus create a living legacy. A seventy-one-year-old widow came to me and said she wanted coaching. She said her husband had died two years earlier and he had left her plenty of money to live without worry, but she felt something was missing. She wanted something meaningful in her life.

After some inquiry and asking a few apt powerful questions, I began to explore ideas with her. I asked her, "Are there any dreams you have given up on or put on hold from earlier in your life?" There was a long silence. She looked deep in reverie and then said "yes."

"As a young girl, I had loved dance: ballet, jazz, and ballroom, just any kind. But I got pregnant at age twenty. I then devoted myself to my assumed homemaker duties, taking care of the kids, my husband, and the household. My dreams of dance got shelved and forgotten."

She had not been asked these types of questions before, and I could see in her eyes and hear in her voice the younger woman she remembered. This was touching something deep within her. She was not incapable of absorbing this revelation, and it did not cause her to be broken in any way. But it did open up a long-buried dream that was truly an expression of her essence.

I asked, "How is dance in your life now? Do you attend dance performances?"

She said "yes, but I sometimes felt sad watching performances because it brings up such a yearning to dance. I feel such envy and loss.

I then asked, "Well, why don't you dance?"

She replied, "You're crazy. I'm too old!"

To be a coach is to believe in endless possibilities tempered with a dash of reality. I asked if there were dance classes in town that she could go to and enjoy the movement. The eventual outcome for this feisty woman was that she went to dance classes and loved them. Her teacher's feedback was that she was better than women half her age, which of course she enjoyed hearing. But the best part was that she and a couple of younger women, actually in their sixties, formed a troupe that began doing dance recitals and therapy at nursing homes, schools, and churches in her area.

Boldly disclosing to me her cherished dream had opened the door to resuscitating it. At age seventy-one, she rediscovered her dancer's legs and her buoyant heart. We were both overjoyed with her creation, which got written up in the local paper and gave her joy for several more years. She stayed involved with her troupe and the dance world even after her movements became limited. My client had found her legs, just as the Velveteen Rabbit did when he became real.

> But the little Rabbit sat quite still for a moment and never moved. For when he saw all the wild rabbits dancing around him he suddenly remembered about his hind legs, and he didn't want them to see that he was made all in one piece … And he might have sat there a long time, too shy to move, if just then something hadn't tickled his nose, and before he thought what he was doing he lifted his hind toe to scratch it.

> And he found that he actually had hind legs! Instead of dingy velveteen he had brown fur, soft and shiny, his ears twitched by themselves, and his whiskers were so long that they brushed the grass. He gave one leap and the joy of using those hind legs was so great that he went springing about the turf on them, jumping sideways and whirling round as the others did … He was a Real Rabbit at last, at home with the other rabbits.[6]

As you can see by my clients' stories, being willing to be naked in the presence of another, to risk being fully seen, transforms lack into love, emptiness into fullness, and shame into pride. What might be the ultimate results of coming clean? Poetry? Writing? Dance? Stop shying away from your special talents, gifts, and skills. These aspects of ourselves energize our realness and help us dream out loud in the

---

[6] Ibid.

presence of a great listener: a coach, therapist, friend, minister, or family member. Everyone shares the same destiny, to find our own wholeness and share it everywhere.

Make use of the stories and exercises included here to prod and shake what's most alive in you. Find a way to give your dream voice and witness. As Sue Monk Kidd says in *The Invention of Wings*, "There is no pain on earth that doesn't crave a benevolent witness."

Here I introduce you to a process useful for reclaiming parts of your authentic self that you may have left hidden in the shadows. Follow this template for naked sharing slowly, using a journal, personal reflection time, and patience.

- **Recall**: Remember a belief or experience that causes you to keep it hidden.
- **Reflect**: Consider this memory. What happened? Who was there? How did it affect you?
- **Reveal on paper**: Write in a journal your memories, thoughts, feelings, actions, and emotional reactions. Just free flow. Get it out and on paper. Then read it to yourself as if you were hearing about it from your younger self.
- **Reveal to another**: Make a big step. Who can you share your story with? Who can you trust will listen to you with suspended judgment and full acceptance?
- **Reboot**: After you have shared with a trusted other, imagine you are rebooting your memory, just like a computer memory. Let it be defragmented and safely put away.
- **Restart**: Get back on your journey to your future, starting now. You have now achieved a clean restart pertaining to this memory or story.

Now you have found ways to begin to reveal your truths, first to your self and then to another. In the next chapter, you will discover the value of playfulness and fun in a life well lived.

# Chapter 3

# 50 Shades of Play: How to Have Fun While Seriously Living

"Don't die with your music still inside you. Listen to your intuitive inner voice and find what passion stirs your soul. Listen to that inner voice, and don't get to the end of your life and say, 'What if my whole life has been wrong?'"

—Ralph Waldo Emerson

We all have a need to have fun, but without hurting others through biting sarcasm, which is a clue to something hidden. Good humor is jovial, energizing, and attractive. If you experience humor at others' expense or even have overly self-deprecating humor, it is a clue to something that could be explored more deeply in order to achieve more wholeness.

Comedians often come from dysfunctional or sad and lonely childhoods, which they have turned into comedy. The best transcend. The others are funny on stage but not funny nor happy in their lives of drugs, depression, emptiness, and so forth. How does play and fun help us transcend what has been transgressed?

I believe we all can learn to lighten up, to take life seriously while not always being serious, a paradox worth exploring. Many stories from children's books bring nostalgic memories to our mind, but I believe many of these tales that are classics also contain much wisdom for adults. They help us in connecting to the art of whimsy and playfulness.

> The Caterpillar and Alice looked at each other for some time in silence: at last the Caterpillar took the hookah out of its mouth, and addressed her in a languid, sleepy voice.
>
> "Whoooooo are YOU?" said the Caterpillar.
>
> This was not an encouraging opening for a conversation. Alice replied, rather shyly, "I--I hardly know, sir, just at present—at least I know who I WAS when I got up this morning, but I think I must have been changed several times since then."
>
> "What do you mean by that?" said the Caterpillar sternly. 'Explain yourself!"
>
> "I can't explain MYSELF, I'm afraid, sir" said Alice, "because I'm not myself, you see."
>
> "I don't see," said the Caterpillar.
>
> "I'm afraid I can't put it more clearly," Alice replied very politely, "for I can't understand it myself to begin with; and being so many different sizes in a day is very confusing."[7]

That passage from one of my favorite all-time books is one of many that makes me smile and remember poignant and profound times as a child of make-believe and imagination.

---

[7]   Lewis Carroll, *Alice's Adventures in Wonderland* (Macmillan, 1865).

## The Value of Play: Can It Coexist with Work?

"Too much fun at work." That is something I rarely hear these days in my profession of coaching people on living their best lives. Yet I wonder if we don't discount the value of enjoyment for high performance on the job. There is power in play, even for the most serious of careers.

Studies show that play creates a survival advantage in the wild.[8] When young animals engage in rough-and-tumble pretend-fighting or play, they are learning skills and social rules. Those that play the most grow more neurons and have more robust mental as well as physical stamina.

Humans also benefit from play during their entire life span, not just as children and adolescents. In older adults, those who engage in the most cognitive activity—doing puzzles, reading, or engaging in mentally challenging work—have a 63 percent lower chance of getting Alzheimer's disease than the general population do. Adults who continue to explore and learn throughout life are less prone to dementia and less likely to get heart disease. The people who stay sharp and interesting as they age are the ones who continue to play and work.

According to Stuart Brown, MD, author of *Play: How It Shapes the Brain, Opens the Imagination and Invigorates the Soul*, posits that the opposite of work is not play. Play and work are mutually supportive. Yet most of us have learned to be serious when it comes to our careers. We squelch our natural drive to have fun.

Play is not the enemy of work. In fact, neither can thrive without the other. We need the newness of play, the sense of flow, imagination, and energy of being in the moment. We also need the sense of purpose in work: the economic stability it provides, the sense of meaning, and competence. The quality that work and play have in common is creativity. In both we are creating new relationships and skills and making things happen.

Often an overwhelming sense of responsibility and competitiveness can bury our inherent need for variety and challenge. If we deny our

---

[8]  http://en.wikipedia.org/wiki/Play_%28activity%29

need to play, we will eventually fall to stress and burn out. Recognizing our biological need for play can transform work. Play helps us deal with difficulties, handle challenges, and tolerate routines and emotions such as boredom or frustration. Play provides a sense of expansiveness, promotes mastery, and remains vital to the creative process.

Whatever happened to unbridled joy in our daily lives? Remember the fun of play as children? Nearly everyone starts out in life playing quite naturally with whatever is available. We make up rules, invent games with playmates, fantasize, and imagine mysteries and treasures.

Maybe we need to renew ourselves more through purposeful play. Something happens to most of us as we become working adults. We shift our priorities into organized, competitive, goal-directed activities. If an activity doesn't teach us a skill, make us money, or further our social relationships, we don't want to waste time being nonproductive.

Sometimes the sheer demands of daily living and family responsibilities seem to rob us of the ability to play.

> I have found that remembering what play is all about and making it part of our daily lives are probably the most important factors in being a fulfilled human being. The ability to play is critical not only to being happy, but also to sustaining social relationships and being a creative, innovative person.[9]

Dr. Stuart Brown, founder of the National Institute for Play, presents his ideas on this TED TV video, *Play Is More than Fun*. Sprinkled with anecdotes demonstrating the play habits of subjects from polar bears to corporate CEOs, Brown promotes play at every age while defining it thus, "Play is an absorbing, apparently purposeless activity that provides enjoyment and a suspension of self-consciousness and sense of time. It is also self-motivating and makes you want to do it again."

We tend to underestimate the power of play. Imagine a world without it, not only the absence of games or sports but also the missing presence

---

[9]   Stuart Brown, MD, *Play: How It Shapes the Brain, Opens the Imagination and Invigorates the Soul* (Scribe Publications, 2009).

of movies, arts, music, jokes, and dramatic stories. No daydreaming, teasing, or flirting. Play lifts people out of the routine of the mundane and offers a means to find joy in even the little things.

Adults who continue to explore and learn throughout life are less prone to develop dementia and heart disease. The people who stay sharp and interesting as they age continue to play and work. When we stop playing, we stop growing. And we will not experience vital aging, but death waiting.

**Play at Work**

It's obvious that play outside of work—via sports, games, family activities, and community functions—is essential. What is less obvious is our need to play at work as we work. Play as we work can energize and help us to see new patterns. It sparks curiosity and triggers ideas and innovation.

Play helps us deal with work problems. What kind of play is appropriate at work? You don't have to engage in off-site team-building games to play at work, although those are occasionally beneficial. A playful attitude gives people the emotional distance to rally. Often the problem is not the problem. It's how we react to the problem.

Play is a lubricant that allows individuals to be close to one another. When we play, we don't put up defensive walls. We accept others as they are. We have a responsibility to play fair. When our interactions are based on a foundation of caring, we avoid hurting others.

Play enables cooperative socialization and nourishes trust, empathy, caring, and sharing. Perhaps one of the biggest advantages to those with a playful mind-set is that it stimulates creativity. Playfulness leads to imagination, inventiveness, and dreams, which help us think up new solutions to problems.

> Play is what allows us to attain a higher level of existence,
> new levels of mastery, imagination, and culture. When

we play right, all areas of our lives go better. When we ignore play we start having problems.[10]

My personal motto is, "If it isn't fun, I don't want to do it. And when it isn't, how can I make it fun?" Try that and let me know how it impacts your life. With my view of the importance, if not necessity or getting naked (emotionally) on occasion with the proper precautions, I also believe that incorporating and actually being purposeful about play in your life can help.

Playfulness, for me, is a mind-set and intention of having fun in a way that is not at the expense of others or even as a self-deprecating way of putting yourself or others in a negative light. Comedians, who often have tragic pasts, use humor about others and themselves as a way to get laughs but often hide their true tragic or hurtful existence in many cases.

My hope for you, the reader, is to find ways to have fun and be lighthearted when life hands you circumstances that may be challenging. This does not mean to make light of tragedy or hurts, but eventually when time has passed and you have shined the light on the emotional scars from such an event, you might be able to smile or laugh at the paradox of living a human life.

Life is not always funny, but eventually acceptance comes from finding vitality from living with a *joie de vivre* (joy of living), an exuberant enjoyment of life.

## An Executive's Story

Some years ago, I was referred a top-level executive in the financial services, a female who was a vice president with international duties from a major U.S. corporation. She had received what is called a 360-degree assessment from her staff and those who report to her, which is a tool that is anonymous but useful to receive honest feedback about your

[10] Stuart Brown, MD, *Play: How It Shapes the Brain, Opens the Imagination and Invigorates the Soul.*

leadership style, teamwork, and perceptions of your effectiveness and personality too.

My client read the summaries and shared with me that many of her team reports have stated she got good results but seemed "reserved, calculating, unfriendly, and stern." She said she was not surprised, but she wanted to change that view and asked for coaching to assist.

In my history taking of her past, I learned she was an above average student, went to prestigious schools, and was also a concert pianist from a young age.

But when speaking of the music skills, she became emotional and said, "I was good, but I never enjoyed it."

She had been forced to practice and perform by her parents, who sought for her to express her skill, but they were very demanding and stern in the process.

I asked what else about her early childhood or adolescence could she remember that was joyful, outside of her academics and music.

There was a long pause and a sigh. She finally said, "I don't remember having much fun or playing with other kids. I was busy with my schoolwork, music lessons, and practice, and I felt disconnected." As I allowed her to sit with that thought, she sighed and paused again. "Wow! That's sad, isn't it?"

I asked, "What was fun for her today? How had she found ways to experience and express joy?"

She then responded, "I experience joy from my leadership role and the creative outcomes, and I enjoy going to art showings and other activities with a few friends or someone whom I am dating.

I silently thought, "This woman needs to find a way to have childlike fun, laughter, and unplanned, spontaneous enjoyment."

But as a coach, I did not tell her that. I just explored my thinking with a request. I then asked her "what experiences have you had around children, either in the past or present time.?"

She had no children of her own; nor did she have any pets. She reported that "my five-year-old niece sometimes comes over with my sister, and I really enjoy watching her."

I then asked "what do you like about that?" and she said "my niece just has fun with nothing and anything. She makes up stories to act out. She plays with My Little Pony and other children's toys. But she also makes friends quickly with other kids when we got to the park or the zoo."

That's when I had a creative idea, which often happens in coaching once intuition kicks in. I asked, "Would you would consider an odd request?"

And she, of course, trusting me, said, "Well, it depends."

I asked, "would you be willing to go to a nearby park and observe the children for at least an hour? Just sit on the bench and have a book or a lunch, and just observe and notice how kids play and interact with joyful exuberance. Would you do that?" (Truthfully I had no idea what I sought or what might happen, but I felt it was worth the experiment.)

She agreed, and the next week, our session was one of a great breakthrough. She came on the call, and after some pleasantries to settle in, I asked, "How did the experiment in the park go?"

There was a pause and then a giggle. And then she said, "You are not going to believe what happened."

Intrigued, I said, "Please say more."

After an hour of watching and observing, she felt a strange urge to get on one of the swings and just swing. When she did that, the nearby kids chuckled, and some came to push her, as an adult would do to a kid. Laughing and swinging, she was having no sense of being a proper adult. She was being childlike and freely playing. She then went to the park on another day over her lunch break, and some of the same kids greeted her. She said she had a sense of belonging and feeling accepted in a way she never had.

The end result of this story is that the playful personality carried over to work. She began being warmer to her staff, asking about their families, looking at photos of their kids or grandkids, and showing a newfound appreciation of the lessons from children in playfulness. She told me that opened her up to a willingness to be childlike at times, but not childish.

Months later, her staff gave her feedback about how much more fun she was. Even though she was still the boss, she was more respected. And she was promoted to a job in Asia as a result, which she had always wanted.

## Aging and a Playful Viewpoint

Another stage of life other than our work persona is the social aspect of our various life experiences. Now that I am in my wise elder years, having lived a long and adventure-filled life, I witness many around me who are also in their sixties, seventies, eighties, and even nineties who live with a zest and a vitality that I think has been a key component in such a long life.

Now I also live in a multi-age community and love hearing the young children as they get off the school bus or as they play and laugh so uninhibitedly, a lesson for all of us. However, the older citizens I socialize with that have a vitality of living do something playful!

My wife and I play tennis four to five times a week for ninety-minute doubles matches. (She's with women, I'm with the men, and one day, we're with couples.) And it's all for fun. Even though it is competitive and robust, no one remembers the score later. It's just fun!

And I compete with some seventy- and eighty-year-old active adults that make me hope I am able to be so mobile when I reach that age. We also laugh a lot, but not at each other. It's at the play itself when funny things happen, as the unpredictability of tennis shots are often part of the fun, even for skillful players. For others it might be dance, art, or other sports. Whatever is fun.

The story of Rose is a reminder that playfulness and joyfulness create blessings for all.

## The Story of Rose

The story of Rose is entitled "Never Too Old to Live Your Dream." It was written by Dan Clark and published in the 1999 book, *Chicken*

*Soup for the College Soul: Inspiring and Humorous Stories about College.* It was later republished in several later *Chicken Soup* books.

> The first day of school, our professor introduced himself and challenged us to get to know someone new. I stood up to look around, when a gentle hand touched my shoulder. I turned around to find a wrinkled, little old lady beaming up at me with a smile that lit up her entire being.
>
> She said, "Hi, handsome. My name is Rose. I'm 87 years old. Can I give you a hug?"
>
> I laughed and enthusiastically responded, "Of course you may!" and she gave me a giant squeeze.
>
> "Why are you in college at such a young, innocent age?" I asked. She jokingly replied, "I'm here to meet a rich husband, get married, have a couple of children, and then retire and travel."
>
> "No, seriously," I asked. I was curious as to what motivated her to take on this challenge at her age.
>
> "I always dreamed of having a college education, and now I'm getting one!" she told me.
>
> After class, we walked to the student union building and shared a chocolate milkshake. We became instant friends. Every day for the next three months, we would leave class together and talk nonstop. I was always mesmerized listening to this "time machine" as she shared her wisdom and experience. Over the course of the year, Rose became a campus icon and easily made friends. She loved to dress up, and reveled in the attention bestowed on her by the other students. She was living it up.

At the end of the semester, we invited Rose to speak at our football banquet. I'll never forget what she taught us. She was introduced and stepped up to the podium. As she began to deliver her prepared speech, she dropped her 3 x 5 cards on the floor. Frustrated and a little embarrassed, she leaned into the microphone and simply said, "I'm sorry I'm so jittery. I gave up beer for Lent, and this whiskey is killing me! I'll never get my speech back in order, so let me just tell you what I know." As we laughed, she cleared her throat and began.

We do not stop playing because we are old; we grow old because we stop playing. There are only four secrets to staying young. One is being happy. Another is achieving success. You also have to laugh and find humor every day. And you've got to have a dream. When you lose your dreams, you die. We have so many people walking around who are dead and don't even know it!

There is a huge difference between growing older and growing up. If you are 19 years old and lie in bed for one full year and don't do one productive thing, you will turn 20 years old. If I am 87 years old and stay in bed for a year and never do anything, I will turn 88. Anybody can grow older. That doesn't take any talent or ability. The idea is to grow up by always finding the opportunity in change.

Have no regrets. The elderly usually don't have regrets for what we did, but rather for the things we did not do. The only people who fear death are those with regrets. She concluded her speech by courageously singing "The Rose," made famous by Bette Midler. She challenged each of us to study the lyrics and live them out in our daily lives.

At the year's end, Rose finished the college degree she had begun all those years ago. One week after graduation, Rose died peacefully in her sleep. Over 2,000 college students attended her funeral in tribute to the wonderful woman who taught, by example, it is never too late to be all you can possibly be.

Remember, growing old is mandatory; growing up is optional.

Self-styled psycho-neuro-immunologist Paul Pearsall, who I met several times, contends that we often think with our hearts rather than our heads. He wrote in *The Heart's Code: Tapping the Wisdom and Power of our Heart Energy* that we humans have a cellular memory. But the wisdom he most expressed in a couple of presentations I heard was that laughter increases the health of our heart and our physical system in general. Whether right or wrong, he stated that seven good belly laughs each day led to an increase in endorphins and influenced a healthier body-mind system.

Norman Cousins' account of healing through laughter was described in his groundbreaking book, *Anatomy of an Illness as Described by the Patient*, which inspired research into the effect of emotions on health that continues to this day. When he was ill with a chronic condition and watched comedic movies over and over, he reported how the laughter improved his health.

Dr. Patch Adams, famously played by Robin Williams in the movie, was famous for being a doctor with expressive humor as part of his treatment approach. He once stated,

> Remember laughing? Laughter enhances the blood flow to the body's extremities and improves cardiovascular function. Laughter releases endorphins and other natural mood elevating and pain-killing chemicals, improves the transfer of oxygen and nutrients to internal organs. Laughter boosts the immune system and helps the body fight off disease, cancer cells as well as viral, bacterial and other infections. Being happy is the best cure of all diseases!

In *Gesundheit!* Dr. Patch Adams reminds medical providers, "Your goal is not to hurt people or belittle suffering, but to bring fun to those who are suffering."

As George Bernard Shaw stated, "We don't stop playing because we grow old; we grow old because we stop playing."

So what do you do for fun? What would you like to do that you are not? How often do you laugh? What dreams have you given up on that may be adaptable today? Who can you share with what you haven't shared about silly ideas? What would you do if having fun were the only criteria? The following are some suggestions:

1. Watch funny YouTube videos that make you laugh and smile. There are many.
2. Find a playmate. Who can you invite to do fun things with?
3. Make a playdate. Schedule spontaneity, and decide to have fun on purpose.
4. Laugh more. There is even training in Laughing Yoga. Google it, and giggle with it.
5. Be a kid again. Research has shown, once you immerse yourself in kidlike environments, it impacts your mind and body. Fly a kite, swing on swings, play tag, and throw balls and Frisbees. Find some kids from your friends and family to hang around, and learn to remember play.
6. Don't sweat the small stuff. As the late Richard Carson famously said in ***Don't Sweat the Small Stuff***, "It's all small stuff!"
7. Write in your journal. Then find someone to get naked with about your insights and things you can share that will make your life more playful.

Now, taking lightness of being with you, I encourage you to now learn more about the shadow of your life and what it holds both in dark secrets, but also wonderful possibilities that have not been in full view.

# Chapter 4

# Your Shadow: Don't Leave Home Without It

"Who looks outside dreams; who looks inside awakens."

—Carl Jung

In my graduate education in psychology, I enthusiastically studied the theories and writings of Carl Jung, a Swiss psychoanalyst with whom I shared the interest in his transpersonal views of human nature and theories of higher consciousness. Jung, to me, was able to express the human condition without ignoring the spiritual aspect of higher realms of consciousness, or what Maslow later called the "farther reaches of human nature."

One of the less esoteric principles of Jung's theories—and one that has influenced generations of therapists, consultants, and self-help teachers and seekers—is the concept of the shadow. The shadow side of our personality, for many, is wrongly accused of holding only our deep, dark secrets, or human tendencies to be other than good and gracious. This is somewhat true, but the shadow also holds all the uniquely brilliant and creative aspects of our self, if we let some light shine on it, allowing a more complete and authentic human experience.

## Understanding Your Shadow Self

Perhaps one of the least understood and most powerful concepts in personal and spiritual development is the shadow. In the world of self-help, where so-called experts are found by the thousands and spiritually hungry and uninformed consumers eagerly seek and gobble up unproven hyperbole accompanied by often useless advice, there is a concept that does not receive the attention that I believe it deserves, your shadow self.

And here's the truth: either you own your shadow, or it owns you. You can try to ignore, hide, or deny it, but until you embrace and make friends with it, you will be missing the key to optimal living as the shadow contains what needs to be unlocked and freed, both what is holding you back and what will propel you forward to a more fulfilling existence.

Jung wrote in 1963, (Collected Works of Carl Jung, volume 9)

> The shadow is that hidden, repressed, for the most part inferior and guilt-laden personality whose ultimate ramifications reach back into the realm of our animal ancestors and so comprise the whole historical aspect of the unconscious (Diamond, 96)[11]. The shadow is a primordial part of our human inheritance, which, try as we might, can never be eluded.

> But the view I want you to consider is that it is so much more ... as I have tried to emphasize, what is also hidden in the darkness are the uniquely creative and parts of who you are to yet be revealed. It is a yin/yang relationship of good and bad, powerful and scary ... But it is just the shadow ... and archetype that is not real, a metaphor that can be useful, rather than constraining.[12]

---

[11] https://www.psychologytoday.com/blog/evil-deeds/201204/essential-se...could Post published by Stephen A Diamond Ph.D.

[12] Connie Zweig and Jeremiah Abrams, eds., *Meeting the Shadow: The Hidden Power of the Dark Side of Human Nature* (New York: Jeremy P. Tarcher/Putnam, 1991).

Instead of the popular phrase *process of elimination*, I prefer to think instead of shadow work as the *process of illumination*.

## Peter Pan's Shadow

I have very vivid memories of the 1953 film *Peter Pan*, which I must have seen a dozen times. In the film, while Peter was visiting the Darling household to listen to the oldest daughter read bedtime stories, the Darling's dog Nana barked at the intruder, and while Peter escaped, his shadow was captured. That night, Wendy Darling discovered Peter's shadow and stored it in her drawer to prevent it from getting into trouble. The next night, Peter and Tinker Bell returned to retrieve it. Once they found it, they accidentally woke Wendy. As Peter attempted to restore it with soap, Wendy preferred the proper way and sewed it back.

And it seems that both he and his shadow have a playful personality. Before it was reattached to him, the shadow had frequently played with Peter Pan by being separated and free and teasing Peter. Though after being sewed back up, the shadow is now again part of Peter. This, of course, is at the same time of the story where Peter is supposed to be maturing even though he does not want to ever grow up.

There are many ways to view this metaphor of the shadow, but suffice it to say, we are not complete if not integrated with our shadow. It must be seen as attached for permanence and not denied or ignored in a way that will interrupt the integration of the personality, or what Jung called *individuation*, the process of psychological integration.

Jung also regarded individuation as a solution to what he considered one of the major problems facing modern people: how to link up consciousness to the unconscious and how to bring our ego mind (consciousness) into a working relationship with our inner *terra incognita*, our unknown inner terrain.

In addition to the concept of shadow, we might also consider the use of masks, disguising our true self at various ages and stages of life. This concept significantly parallels the writing of Joseph Campbell in his famous *The Hero with a Thousand Faces.* This book has influenced the writings and creation of many a famous storyteller, filmmaker, and artists. *The Wizard of Oz, Star Wars,* King Arthur, *The Hobbit,* Harry Potter, and Homer's *Odyssey* are all about the hero's journey. This mythical journey includes rites of passage of the hero, his quest, the magic elixirs or swords (or light sabers), and the search for the way back home in the end, the way back to self but changed somehow.

Campbell's thinking runs parallel to that of Jung, who wrote much about archetypes, universal and constantly recurring themes and characters that occur in the dreams of all people and the myths of all cultures. Archetypes include the following: the wise, old person; the warrior; the hero; and others. Jung suggested that these archetypes are reflections of various aspects of the human mind and a collective unconscious we tap into, where our personality divides into these characters to play out the drama of our life.

Our problem, though, is we sometimes act as if the drama is real, forgetting we are making up our story, conceptualizing our narrative about the drama of our life as if we are the only one faced with such a story of human challenges. If we don't learn to share authentically with a few or even just one trusting individual, we live our life with a drawer full of masks and a detached shadow leaving us to be incomplete.

It is important to also not forget that the shadow seen only as the dark and scary parts of our psyche denies the wonderfully unique aspects of our unique birth on this planet and the gifts, dreams, and aspirations we bring with us or discover along our journey. In my coaching, I often ask my clients if there is a dream they have given up on, and although maybe it cannot be realized now as it could have been, the yearning is still there for expression of that unique calling or personality aspect.

What greatness in you is unspoken, undiscovered? Human development, in my view, is more about discovering than it is uncovering and recovering. Too often we have created a view that we must have something wrong with us. We begin to engage in personal archeology and dig up and then rebury our deep secrets that don't fit the narrative we live with.

I instead want to shed light on the positive and unrealized aspects. Come out into the light. Your shadow is with you all the time, even when the sun is not shining. Perhaps that is what enlightenment is, shining the light on what could be rather than what was.

Eric Hoffer recognized how easy it is for us humans to get in our own way. Hoffer, an American social philosopher, authored ten books. He was awarded the Presidential Medal of Freedom in February 1983. His first book, *The True Believer* (1951), was widely recognized as a classic, receiving critical acclaim from both scholars and laypersons alike. Despite rising to fame with the success and popularity of his writings, he continued to work as a longshoreman until retiring at age sixty-five. My father gave me a copy to read as a young teen, and I have kept this quote in my quotation box ever since. Hoffer once said, "Our greatest pretenses are built up not to hide the evil and the ugly in us, but our emptiness. The hardest thing to hide is something that is not there." (Eric Hoffer, *The Passionate State of Mind*, 1955)

**What Is the Shadow?**

The shadow is comprised of those aspects of your self that are hidden away in the dark and out of your everyday awareness. Many of these aspects of your self have grips on your life and actually impact your thoughts, feelings, beliefs, and behaviors. A metaphor would be that of a secret chamber where you keep those parts of yourself that, at least on an unconscious level, you would rather avoid or ignore and even try to forget them.

The shadow includes your long-hidden fears, shames, regrets, judgments, beliefs, and also your greatest strengths, dreams, and divine and sacred self. In other words, the shadow includes all these things about yourself that "you don't know that you don't know" or those things that Jung and others believe reside in your subconscious. But I say, if you learn to find the right way, time, and person to help you explore, it doesn't have to be as scary as you might think. And there are also precious gems and treasures hidden as well! These might be dreams you have given up on or long-lost ideas of how to live your life. Yet they may still inform you today about parts of you from which you may feel disconnected and also give you a frequent sense of something missing.

## The Importance of Embracing and Exploring Your Shadow

With the understanding that your everyday experience, including relationships, career, money, health, or parenting, is a reflection of your inner state, the shadow, of course, has a great impact on how you live your life. The shadow is an important part of your inner self that is hidden from your awareness. Avoiding, denying, or ignoring your shadow is like knowing that a part of you is missing but fearing that it is too scary or overwhelming to let out of the castle. Yet befriending your shadow is like pulling back the curtain (as Toto did to the Wizard of Oz) and revealing the programming that dictates your thoughts, feelings, and behaviors and eventually your choices and outcomes in life.

In addition to taking back the power from those parts of you that hold you back from achieving your desired results, getting familiar with and embracing your shadow can assist you in unleashing trapped life energies, your unexpressed personal power, inspiration, and authenticity. For example, many people know they are extremely talented; however, their life stories do not reflect this fact.

Can you see how much energy is put into keeping yourself small although it does not serve you or those exact people you try to protect? Can you see how much of your life force is suffocated? Honoring these old truths, beliefs, and fears that served you in the past and then releasing their hold on you can free much of your energy and inner power to be used to achieve both progress in your daily life and desired results you seek.

Here are a few ways to bring some of your shadow material into the light:

1. Examine any long-held stories of some shameful, guilt-producing, or fearful event or experiences from the past. You

may find, once shared in a new light, the power holding on to you will begin to dissipate. Our memories and fears are usually blown out of proportion and no longer serve us after we have moved on from whatever happened.

2. Please consider that the things you perceive as faults, negative patterns, or things you do not like about yourself are actually your assets. The only issue with them is that they are overamplified. If you turn the volume down a little, these so-called faults can become strengths. This kind of examination will assist you in revealing hidden fears, beliefs, and even vows you have made that can be called on to be honored for their past service and then released.

3. Make a list in a personal journal of those things you would find it difficult to reveal about yourself or any long-held beliefs about something you have attached to shame, guilt, or fear.

If you could find someone who you could share this with to just clear it out of your hiding place, who might that person be? A therapist? A trusted friend? A spiritual advisor? A life coach? What would it take for you to imagine having that conversation? What would be a positive outcome to such a sharing?

The following is a helpful format for beginning to practice self-disclosure and cleaning out what's hidden in the shadows that are stealing power from you living fully and authentically. Try it! Get real. Be authentic. Be courageous. Make contact, listen well, and empathize. Trust and self-disclose, and invite others to do the same. Find people and places where you can say what you really need to share, not to fix it or change it, but just to share it out loud with a caring listener.

What we worry about, remain anxious about, or are hurt by is never in the moment of now. It either comes from our past and the perceptions that create our narrative or the future, which is just made up. It hasn't happened yet.

You can embrace even the difficult memories or experiences in your life and the fears you have of what may come and also begin to find the joy and expansiveness in the truly bright spots and unique gifts you bring to this earth and its inhabitants. Learn the value of being wholehearted but the additional value of being whole-spirited. You are unique, and you are needed to be real. So invite those special people in your life to be real as well.

We have all learned to wear masks and protective armor from a young age and rightfully so. The world is not a place to be vulnerable all the time. But if we never let down our guard or take off the masks and the armor, we never really feel free and whole

**Take Action Template** (introduced in chapter 1)

- **Recall:** Remember a belief or experience that causes you to keep it hidden.
- **Reflect:** Consider this memory. What happened? With whom did it occur? How did it affect you then? How has it continued to affect you?
- **Reveal on paper**: In a journal, write your memories, thoughts, feelings, actions, and emotional reactions. Just free flow. Get it out and on paper. Then read it to yourself as if you were hearing about it from your younger self. Write a story, poem, or free association mind dump. Just get it out of your head and your heart.
- **Reveal to another**: Make a big step. Who can you share your story with? Who can you trust will listen to you with suspended judgment and full acceptance? You might burn it, bury it in your yard, or tie it to a balloon and send it off in the sky.
- **Reboot**: After you have shared with a trusted other, imagine you are rebooting your memory, just like a computer. Let it be defragmented, and safely put away. Imagine that you have created new, clean space to really experience life refreshed.
- **Restart**: Get back on your journey to your future, starting now. You have now achieved a clean restart pertaining to this memory or story. Step into your future, and live it.

As is written in the book of changes (*I Ching*), "It is only when we have the courage to face things as they are without any self-deception or illusion that a light will develop out of events by which the path to success may be recognized."

Having become more familiar with your shadow and hopefully finding its exploration less scary, you can now see how the concept of transparency shows up in our work roles, in both healthy and unhealthy ways.

# Chapter 5

# The Emperor's New Clothes: Transparency in Our Work Roles

You might be familiar with the classic story of *The Emperor's New Clothes*, a short tale by Hans Christian Andersen about a vain emperor who cares about nothing except wearing and displaying opulent clothes. He hires two swindlers who promise him the finest, best suit of clothes from a fabric invisible to anyone who is either unfit for his position or hopelessly stupid. The emperor's ministers cannot see the clothing themselves but pretend they can for fear of appearing unfit for their positions, and the emperor does the same. Finally the swindlers report that the suit is finished. They mime dressing him, and the emperor marches in procession before his subjects. The townsfolk play along with the pretense, not wanting to appear unfit for their positions or stupid. Then a child in the crowd, too young to understand the desirability of keeping up the pretense, blurts out that the emperor is wearing nothing at all, and others take up the cry. The emperor cringes, suspecting the assertion is true, but continues the procession. The tale has been translated into over a hundred languages.[13]

There are many angles from which one can look at that story in the modern world in which we live today. There have been well-documented narratives from politics to sports to corporate fraud or to

---

[13] https://en.wikipedia.org/wiki/The_Emperor%27s_New_Clothes

rule-breaking or abusive behaviors. And yet many of those around them pretend the emperor is still dressed. They follow along, protect, deny, and sometimes truly believe all is acceptable.

In the tale, only the child (the innocent) spoke the truth, and yet only some viewed the truth. Others continued acting as if the emperor were clothed in case the clothes really could only be seen by those who were worthy.

In today's workplace, companies that thrive seem to have a better demonstration of collaborative expectations, a value of transparency, and what is called *emotional intelligence.*

Granted, we can all think of examples from corporate emperors or politicians' peccadillos in the news that do not exemplify the best example of honest, open, and trustworthy communication. I do witness in my coaching practice and those of other colleagues examples of companies today (large or small) embracing more honesty and respect for the individual in the workplace. Understandings of emotional adjustments to life challenges are not ignored, even though the bottom line is the job still has to be done.

Rather than pretending the emperor has clothes, real feelings and life experiences are acknowledged with empathy and caring. We used to hear the phrase, "Don't bring your work to home," which means don't bring job frustrations home to your family. And the opposite message, "Don't bring your home to work," was also the assumption from the management. Today personal challenges have a way to be shared and combatted, and programs in wellness, coaching, leadership agility, resilience training, and emotional intelligence meet those challenges head-on with some helpful strategies. It is not that the workplace needs to become a place where all emotions and issues are shared, but also there are times when they need not be kept to oneself when obvious in their impact.

Today the wise companies know there must be an outlet or a service to allow emotional nakedness in the workplace, whether using an Employee Assistance Professional (EAP counselor or coach) or a manager with training in empathic listening and providing an avenue to services that will head off the personal issue before it grows into something larger and destructive.

A recent review of blogs and other postings about today's workplace reveals a new emphasis on transparency, vulnerability, and, of course, authenticity. More honest sharing is valued in today's workplace. There is, however, a subtle distinction between being emotional and wanting or asking others to hold those emotions for you. A colleague could let others know they might be having a tough day, yet if coworkers feel they are walking on eggshells to be careful not to set you off, you have not shared the vulnerability nor been authentic. Enough honesty about a circumstance (work-related or just personal) can be shared without expressing details and asking for anything more than understanding. The key to being vulnerable at work is discovering how to share just enough of what may be emotionally charged without sharing the whole story. Your coworkers will feel honored to be trusted enough for you to share and inspired by how well you manage emotions in challenging times, a mark of emotional intelligence. Transparency at work is honestly sharing things you or others may notice or intuit, but in a way that is appropriate to the reality of the business atmosphere. Truthfulness allows others to relax, and it also does not allow the proverbial elephant in the room. Being naked at those moments is a way of being real with your self and choosing a way to express that truth that fits the moment.

It is somewhat paradoxical that leader vulnerability can actually be one of the most effective ways to engender trust with employees. We are all living at a time when workers want and expect their managers to be more human, less perfect, and, at times, a little vulnerable, regardless of position or authority.

In a book I greatly admire, *Leadership and Self-Deception: Getting Out of the Box* by the Arbinger Institute, written as an allegorical story, an employee learns how his anger and demanding attitude is jeopardizing his job and the functions of his work team and his family as well.

The book is written as a story about a man named Tom who gets some mentoring and coaching from a senior executive named Bud. Tom learns we all have a tendency toward self-deception. And often we don't even know it. We believe what we think we know. And self-deception arises out of putting people in the box. What is the box?

Have you ever wondered if there were a missing ingredient that could make your relationships better in the workplace and your personal life?

When I was introduced to *Leadership and Self-Deception: Getting out of the Box*, I learned that term to be crucial as to why communication can break down at work and how people act in a way that is not beneficial to self or others and pretend the emperor is wearing clothes. Understanding the power of self-deception is not the answer, but it can go a long way in changing the quality and nature of your relationships.

Understanding how acts of self-deception affect our perception and interaction with others is the first step. This awareness can grant us insights into recognizing what we may do and how we do it that leads us to treating people more as objects and not persons with needs and challenges similar to our own.

It is easy to get caught up in the endless doing of work and lose sight of who is at the other end of our interactions. Supervisors or managers, who emphasize results as paramount, can lose their focus seeing interactions among people as tasks rather than dynamic interactions of relationships. Another workplace reality is that we often don't see eye to eye with all of our coworkers, which may lead us to see past their humanness. We put them in the box! So I define self-deception as not knowing—and even resisting the possibility that I might have a problem.

So what is self-deception? Here's one perspective: when we act in ways contrary to what we believe is likely beneficial and appropriate, especially in our relationships, we are then engaging in self-deception. We can deceive ourselves in many ways. We may promise to change our ways, which we never keep. And we may deny our personal self-destructive habits and rationalize behaviors that ignore our inner truths. Moreover, self-deception in relationships is unfortunately common and may become a routine habit if we don't find ways to become more self-aware.

We unconsciously create patterns of thinking, responses to problems, and challenges in our lives, which then leads to developing beliefs that people and events are the root cause of our actions. In other words, we blame others for our actions. We are lying to ourselves.

In truth, our acts of self-deception, primarily unconscious, have a core belief that we fail to see the common humanness in people. We do not readily see how we may be failing to account for the truth that other people all have their own values, needs, wants, and choices that drive their choices in how they are behaving. When we act against our own intrinsic, but ignored, values, we then put ourselves into a box.

## In the Box

According to Arbinger, from the box we see and respond to others through the lens of self-deception. We lose the accurate perception of the other person, and instead to justify our behavior, we blame or find fault with him or her. He or she then becomes a problem, a nuisance, or an obstacle. He or she is no longer a "person" but is objective in some way.

Self-deception is a distorted view that can take many forms. We exaggerate the faults or imperfections of others and emphasize and build up or own virtues. Once we deceive ourselves, we see the other person as the problem and find all the things that we imagine to be wrong about that individual and his or her behavior. Doing so allows us to feel justified in terms of our thoughts and behavior. In other words, we need the other person to be the problem.

And to make matters worse, we often don't even know this may be occurring and we may actually have a problem. Often the common experience is that we carry around our very own boxed-in perspectives, a result of unconscious beliefs, choices, and behavioral expressions. We unknowingly create our own boxes of self-deception. In a very emotion-tugging manner, this wonderful book by Arbinger reveals a new reality that can then lead to more honesty with self and others and a more transparent and honest view of how you reveal yourself in the workplace environment.

If you are a millennial (born after 1980) or work with a millennial, truthfulness and honesty is a strong value. Trust will be earned and rewarded with effort, if truthfulness is present, especially in those they report to or work on teams with.

## JoHari Window

In my years of working as a consultant, trainer, and leadership coach in the corporate environment, a tool I learned about long ago is the JoHari Window. Developed by and created by two American psychologists, Joseph Luft and Harrington Ingham (hence the name JoHari), in 1955, it is a technique used to help people better understand their relationship with themselves as well as others. It has been used primarily in self-help groups and corporate trainings as a discovery process.

More details can be found in many scholarly articles, but for the purposes of this chapter to speak to how to be more authentically transparent and aware in the workplace, I will share how to use the wisdom of this diagram. If you take a look at the four quadrants, which is another way of representing the box concept presented earlier, you can begin to imagine how transparent sharing and truthful dialogue will change the size and shading of the quadrants. This is a very good visual representation of a communication shift that will improve naked relating in the workplace when needed or beneficial. Remember, you don't have to become an open book, but you can unlock the padlocks at times.

Have you ever been part of a group or team at work where everyone was completely open with one another? If you have had that rare experience, you likely worked extremely effectively together. You knew your coworkers very well, and there was a strong sense of trust among you. The result of this positive relationship probably was a high degree of accomplishment and satisfaction with the results that were experienced.

Most of us know that work relationships rely on trust in order to function the best, but how does that trust get built? The Johari Window can assist in understanding how, and it helps you gain new perspectives about yourself and function more authentically as the unique human being you are.

## About the Model

The Johari Window is a visual communication model that can be used to improve understanding among individuals and in groups. This understanding comes from the following shifts in perspective:

1. You can build trust with others by being more self-disclosing and honest.
2. By hearing and considering others' points of view, you can learn about yourself and challenge beliefs or behaviors that are not productive.

The visual perspective of the Johari Window can help coworkers understand the value of appropriate self-disclosure, and you can encourage them to give and accept constructive feedback. Different points of view need to be considered because, even though they may not be true for you, they are for the others.

Experienced in a sensitive and exploratory manner, this tool and process can help workers build better, more trusting relationships with one another, solve issues in collaboration, and work more effectively as a team, while concentrating on strengths and gifts that each member brings.

## Explaining the Johari Window

The Johari Window is shown as a four-quadrant grid, which you can see in the diagram below.

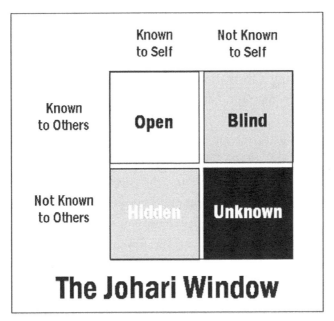

Figure 1. Johari Window.

The four quadrants are:

1. **Open Area (Quadrant 1).** This quadrant represents the things others know about you and the things you know about yourself. This includes your skills, attitudes, behavior, knowledge, and public persona.
2. **Blind Area (Quadrant 2).** This quadrant represents things about you that are known by others but you are not aware of. This can include simple data that you do not know, or it can include buried issues such as feelings of being unworthy, incompetent, or less than, which are often difficult for individuals to face directly and yet can be seen by others.
3. **Hidden Area (Quadrant 3).** This quadrant represents things you know about you but are not known by others.
4. **Unknown Area (Quadrant 4).** This last quadrant represents things that are unknown by both you and others.

## The Desired Outcome

The ultimate goal of the Johari Window is to expand the open area without disclosing information that is too personal. The open area is the most important quadrant. Generally speaking, the more your employees know about each other, the more productive, cooperative, and effective they'll be when working together. The process of enlarging the open area quadrant is called *self-disclosure*, the delicate process of honest sharing that takes place among yourself and the people you're interacting with.

As you share information, your open area expands vertically, and your hidden area gets smaller. As people on your team provide feedback to you about what they know or see about you, your open area expands, and your blind area shrinks. This process of give-and-take, sharing, and open communication (when done well) builds trust within the group.

At first view, the Johari Window may look like a complex tool, but it's actually very easy to comprehend with just a little effort. As such, it provides a visual reference that people can use to look at their own character, and it illustrates the importance of sharing, being open, and accepting feedback from others.

People who have a large open area are usually very easy to be around and to converse with. They communicate honestly and openly with others, and they tend to get along well with a group. People who have a very small open area are difficult to talk to, they seem closed off and uncommunicative, and they often don't work well with others because they haven't shown they can be trusted.

Other people might have a large blind area with many issues they haven't identified or dealt with yet. However, others can see these issues clearly. These people might have low self-esteem, or they may even have other issues of anger or mistrust when working with others.


## Using the Tool

The process of enlarging your open area involves self-disclosure. Put simply, the more you (sensibly) open up and disclose your thoughts, feelings, dreams, and goals, the more you're going to experience trust with your coworkers.

## Remember

Avoid oversharing with your self-disclosure. Disclosing small, harmless items build trust; however, avoid disclosing too much personal information, which could damage people's respect for you.

Another important aspect of enlarging your open area is accepting feedback from others on your team. This feedback helps you learn things about yourself that others can see but you can't. This is important for personal growth.

Be careful in the way you give feedback. Some cultures have a very open and accepting approach to feedback, but others don't. You can cause incredible offense if you offer personal feedback to someone who is not used to it, so be sensitive and start gradually. If someone is interested in learning more about you, he or she can reciprocate by disclosing information in his or her hidden quadrant.

For example, imagine that you tell someone on your team that you're interested in going to business school to get your master's degree. She responds by telling you that she thinks that's a great idea and she just enrolled earlier in the year. She then tells you all about the organizational leadership program that she's enrolled in. You excitedly open up about your career goals, and you discuss how a similar degree will help you on your career path.

In the modern-day workplace, coaching is utilizing theories and practices that have been around quite a while. Theories such as group dynamics, the Johari Window, and tools such as 360 Feedback assessments allow clients to learn about blind spots, their Achilles' heel of behavior tendencies that block effectiveness, and hidden strengths that can be used more effectively. Style assessments or inventories (such as FIRO-B, Meyers-Briggs, and DISC) help people learn how they relate to one another most effectively. All of this has evolved into embracing emotional intelligence as good for business.

The Johari Window is a disclosure/feedback model of self-awareness. This window is a graphical representation of those aspects of our self, which are known or unknown to us and others. It is a model for communication and can also reveal difficulties or challenges. The Johari Window only functions properly with give-and-take of disclosure and feedback, the natural interaction of the coach and coachee. This simple yet effective theory demonstrates the power of the coach offering feedback to the coachee that he or she isn't aware of and working with that person to realize positive change. And by learning to say what has to been said, think what has not been thought, and say it publicly to a supervisor or team, you will feel a bit naked, but today that is acceptable.

Emotional intelligence today is a very popular concept, especially since it has reinforced what everyone always knew but didn't want to admit. Relationships within the workplace are important to the overall success of the company or organization. Businesses improve and show healthier bottom lines if the employees are happier and communicate and function as a team that works well together and resolves conflict early. Emotional intelligence includes personal competence in self-awareness, self-regulation, and motivation as well as social competence in empathy and social skills. Coaching acts as a catalyst in executives and teams to elicit their natural emotional intelligence strengths and promote healthy, functional, and, yes, even enjoyable workplace relationships.

As individual coaching clients obtain results from the various assessment tools and make new and surprising discoveries about themselves, they work with coaches who help them understand the information, determine what changes they want to make, and plan the strategy to reach desired goals. The coach elicits ways that the person can change behaviors. A coach does not tell the person what to do, but instead helps him or her arrive at a strategy for change that he or she had not considered before by evocative questions and supportive possibility thinking. Coaching involves motivational interviewing, powerful questions (discovery), intentional listening, empowerment, consistency, and accountability. As a person's level of confidence and self-esteem rises, it becomes easier to invite others to comment on his or her blind spots. Obviously active and empathic listening skills are important here.

If you don't have a personal coach, use your journal or a trusted friend or mentor and gain some new insights about yourself. It's both exciting and illuminating.

So in pursuing my theme of this chapter of the importance of being able to be naked at appropriate times in the workplace, another concept is very important, *crucial conversations.* There are books and workshops about the skills of learning how to have crucial conversations and are taught to managers in many companies and organizations, including the Pentagon and FBI.

## What Are Crucial Conversations?

When stakes are high and various opinions are expressed, emotions also start to heat up, and casual conversations can quickly move to crucial conversations. The authors of *Crucial Conversations: Tools for Talking When Stakes Are High* state,

> Ironically, the more crucial the conversation, the less likely we are to handle it well. The consequences of either avoiding or fouling up crucial conversations can be severe. When we fail a crucial conversation, every aspect of our lives can be affected—from our careers, to our communities, to our relationships, to our personal health.[14]

Most people benefit once they know a little bit about the research into emotions that derail relationships. This quotation from *Crucial Conversations* exemplifies the heart of the issue: what do people do that jeopardizes relationships?

---

[14] Kerry Patterson, Joseph Grenny, Ron McMillan, and Al Switzler, *Crucial Conversations: Tools for Talking When Stakes Are High* (McGraw-Hill, 2002).

As people begin to feel unsafe, they start down one of two unhealthy paths: move either to silence or violence. Silence almost always is done as a means of avoiding potential problems, and it always restricts the flow of meaning. The three most common forms of silence are masking, avoiding, and withdrawing. Masking consists of understating or selectively revealing our true opinion. Sarcasm, sugarcoating, and couching are some of the more popular forms. Avoiding involves steering completely away from sensitive subjects. We talk but without addressing the real issues. Withdrawing means exiting a conversation altogether. We either exit the conversation or the room.

John Gottman did years of research observing couples to discover what he described as the root behaviors that create toxic relationships. He discovered four behaviors that often send relationships reeling into dysfunction. He called them the *Four Horsemen*: contempt, blaming, stonewalling, and defensiveness. Clients can note behaviors that exemplify the Four Horsemen: silence (usually appearing as masking, avoiding, or withdrawing) and/or violence (usually appearing controlling, labeling, or attacking). Clients benefit once they understand what they do when they display these behaviors and also benefit from understanding how to recognize and limit their impact.

The authors of *Crucial Conversations* follow-up book, *Crucial Accountability: Tools for Resolving Violated Expectations, Broken Commitments, and Bad Behavior,* added the necessary ingredient, accountability. From the back cover, it reads,

> Broken promises, missed deadlines, poor behavior ... they don't just make others' lives miserable; they can sap up to 50 percent of organizational performance and account for the vast majority of divorces. *Crucial Accountability* offers the tool for improving relationships in the workplace and in life and for resolving all these problems ... permanently.[15]

[15] Kerry Patterson, Joseph Grenny, Ron McMillan, Al Switzler, and David Maxfield, *Crucial Accountability: Tools for Resolving Violated Expectations, Broken Commitments, and Bad Behavior* (VitalSmarts, LLC, 2013).

In translation, it means getting naked and being honest, nonjudgmental, and willing to speak your truth and listen to others as well.

Recent research by Leslie K. John, professor of business administration at Harvard Business School, has some interesting findings in this regard. Her research divides responders via a series of compromising scenarios into either revealers or hiders. The results show that 89 percent of participants would hire the revealer over the hider. Similar in a relationship scenario, 64 percent of people would rather date someone who responded as a revealer, a truth teller. Of course, it does not serve us well to use self-disclosure indiscriminately, yet is it imperative that we remain mindful of the implications for withholding what we know or feel. When in doubt, tell the truth.

(Sourced from Harvard Business Review article *The Surprising Benefits of Oversharing* by Michael Blanding, http://hbswk.hbs.edu/item/the-surprising-benefits-of-oversharing)

I have been a member of Rotary International for twenty years of my life and their Four-Way Test, created in 1954, is a good reminder of how to make this real and personal in all endeavors. The Four-Way Test is a nonpartisan and nonsectarian ethical guide for Rotarians to use for their personal and professional relationships. The test has been translated into more than a hundred languages, and Rotarians recite it at club meetings:

Of the things we think, say or do

1. Is it the TRUTH?
2. Is it FAIR to all concerned?
3. Will it build GOODWILL and BETTER FRIENDSHIP?
4. Will it be BENEFICIAL to all concerned?

And another set of useful agreements comes from *The Four Agreements: A Practical Guide to Personal Freedom* by Don Miguel Ruiz.

1. **Be impeccable with your word.** Speak with integrity. Say only what you mean. Avoid using the word to speak against yourself

or to gossip about others. Use the power of your word in the direction of truth and love.

2. **Don't take anything personally.** Nothing others do is because of you. What others say and do is a projection of their own reality, their own dream. Once you are immune to the opinions and actions of others, you won't be the victim of needless suffering.

3. **Don't make assumptions.** Find the courage to ask questions and to express what you really want. Communicate with others as clearly as you can to avoid misunderstandings, sadness, and drama. With just this one agreement, you can completely transform your life.

4. **Always do your best.** Your best is going to change from moment to moment. It will be different when you are healthy as opposed to sick. Under any circumstance, simply do your best, and you will avoid self-judgment, self-abuse, and regret.[16]

In today's workplace, not only is it important, it's also necessary for success to have avenues and opportunities to embrace naked sharing. Employees, including managers and executives, need ways and means (people and places) to get things off their chest and out of the box in order to not pretend that things are different than what may be known but not spoken. If the emperor has no clothes, tell somebody.

And think about both sets of four agreements above as a background to choosing your conversations.

Now, having learned new ways to consider when, and how to be emotionally naked in your work role, the next chapter looks at modern, instantaneous communication with multiple technology, which can range from helpful to disastrous.

---

[16] Don Miguel Ruiz, *The Four Agreements: A Practical Guide to Personal Freedom* (San Rafael, Calif.: Amber-Allen Publishing, Inc., 1997).

# Chapter 6

# From Soup Cans to Cyber Sharing: Modern Communication and Privacy

"Each person's life is lived as a series of conversations."

—Deborah Tanner

"The reality of the other person is not in what he reveals to you, but in what he cannot reveal to you. Therefore, if you would understand him, listen not to what he says but rather to what he does not say."

—Khalil Gibran

Some of you who are wise elders will remember a form of communication we did in our childhoods with two soup cans strung about twenty to thirty feet apart with a string or wire, and we pretended they were phones or communicators of some kind. Really! If you put your ear up while the other was talking, you could hear the voice of the speaker across the string. It was a fun way for young children to pretend.

This was also the time of party line phones when you had to wait for your neighbor to be off so you could make a call. Then as technology sped up, we had sleek designer phones with twenty-foot cords so we could talk where our parents could not hear us (or so we thought) and talk for many minutes to our friends. That was in the 1950s. Then in the 1960s and beyond, look what has changed.

I remember my first fax machine in my psychologist's office as an exciting way to watch a message or document slowly roll out of a base unit with wrinkled paper smelling of ink, waiting for it to dry sometimes. And my first mobile phone looked like the kind soldiers use in the jungles to communicate with base operations. If I had kept every mobile phone I have owned since 1994 or so, I would have a box of cables with different-sized devices and odd-looking adapters. I would also have a lot more money. Now we have cellphones that are ubiquitous and watches as communicators. Remember Dick Tracy? Okay, you young folks are going to have to ask your parents. Or Google it!

Society today worldwide is now just a phone call, text, or message away instantly. And yet the trend of communication via what is called social media has some dire complications and disturbing implications for human communication and living authentically.

Younger people today, millennials, and generation Y (those under forty) are using Facebook, Twitter, and Instagram to share what is sometimes very personal information with photos often included. (I realize there may be new modes and methods by the time you read this.) And the problem with this as I see it is twofold:

1. What's posted on these outlets never goes away in most cases. It's on the Web and in the cloud. You can take it down, delete, or close your profile, but it's still discoverable.
2. This form of communication is not real communication where one can share deeply and meaningfully.

I came across this rap video from an artist named Prince Ea, and it is a very enlightening narrative about the state of our ways of communicating today. In this spoken word piece from Prince Ea, we look at the consciousness of communication, and the American rapper highlights the moments we're missing when we're digitally connected. It's been brought to our attention before, but perhaps with online privacy concerns at an all-time high and a new generation who don't want their online lives archived, probably we're witnessing a rebellious backlash against the general movement to everything stored in the cloud and quantified lives. The following are the lyrics. (I recommend watching the video.)

*Did you know the average person spends 4 years of his life looking down at his cell phone?*
*Kinda ironic ain't it?*
*How these touch-screens can make us lose touch*
*But its no wonder in a world filled with*
*I Mac's, I Pads and I Phones*
*So many I's, so many selfies, not enough Us's and we's*
*See Technology has made us more selfish and separate than ever*
*Cuz while it claims to connect us, connection has gotten no better*
*And let me must express first*
*Mr Zuckerberg, not to be rude but you should re-classify Facebook to what it is:*
*An anti-social network*
*Cuz while we may have big friend lists*
*So many of us are friendless, all alone*
*Cuz friendships and more broken than the screens on our very phones*
*We sit at home on our computers measuring self worth by numbers of followers and Likes*
*Ignoring those who actually love us*
*It seems we'd rather write an angry post*
*Than talk to someone who might actually hug us*
*Am I bugging? You tell me …*
*I asked a friend the other day lets meet up face to face*
*They said alright, what time you wanna Skype?*
*I responded with omg, srs, and then a bunch of smh's*
*And realized what about me?*
*Do I not have the patience to have conversation without abbreviation?*
*This is the generation of media over stimulation*
*Chats have been reduced to snaps*
*The news is 140 characters*

*Videos are 6 seconds at high speed*
*And you wonder why ADD is on the rise faster than 4G LTE*
*But, get a load of this*
*Studies show the attention span of the average adult today*
*Is one second lower than that of a gold fish*
*So if, you're one of the few people or aquatic animals that have yet to*
*click off or close this video, congratulations*
*Let me finish by saying*
*You do have a choice, yes*
*But this ONE my friends we cannot Auto-Correct*
*We must do it Ourself*
*Take control or be controlled, Make a decision*
*ME ...*
*No longer do I want to spoil a precious moment by recording it with*
*a phone*
*I'm just gonna keep them*
*I don't wanna take a picture of all my meals anymore*
*I 'm just gonna eat them*
*I don't want the new app*
*The new software*
*Or the new update*
*And If I wanna post an old photo of myself who says I have to wait*
*until Thursday*
*I'm so tired of performing in the pageantry of vanity*
*And conforming to this accepted form of digital insanity*
*Call me crazy but, I imagine a world where we smile when we have*
*low batteries*
*Cuz that will mean we'll be one bar closer, to Humanity*[17]

As you read or watch this powerful message, think of the deeper meaning. I totally love that I can email people for my business or personal communication asynchronously and let them respond in due

---

[17] http://www.alwaysthinkin.co.uk/prince-ea-asks-us-can-we-auto-correct-humanity

time. I also do love texting because that is the prime method of frequent messages or brief updates from my two daughters. But in the context of this book about being more revealing in the right time with the right people, the message is clear. If we rely on mobile devices and social media for regular communication, our brains will probably turn to silicone-based material in the next generation.

We must take the time to have real communication with those in our life we care about, either in family or business. Facebook is not really face time. It is devoid of real time, in the moment speaking and listening with no eye contact. I do realize that it can be helpful to use applications like Skype or video chat and see the person in real time. But direct phone calls can also work. Real communication takes place in real time. Letter writing, emails, and postings can add to the relationship, but they do not replace the powerful communication of real-time dialogue. The other types of virtual connection can punctuate, share, or just test the waters, but wholehearted speaking and listening need to be in a sacred space with a sacred intention.

The trend for lots of cyber-sharing deeply personal information is a dangerous practice both for untrustworthy people who scour the Internet but also because it is like your childhood diary being shown to the world. TMI, or too much information, it is called today. It's when you want or need to really communicate, find, or develop a few special relationships where you can do that and bare your soul and be naked and safe.

**Today's Generation**

Daughter to Dad: Texting Communication

> Daddy, I am coming home to get married soon. Get out your checkbook. LOL I'm in love with a boy who is far away from me. I am in Australia, and he lives in Scotland. We met on a dating website, became friends on Facebook, had long chats on WhatsApp, he proposed

to me on Skype, and now we've had two months of relationship through Viber. My beloved and favorite Dad, "I need your blessing, good wishes, and a really big wedding." Lots of love and thanks,

Your favorite daughter, Lilly"

Dads reply … also by texting

"My Dear Lilly: Like Wow! Really? Cool! Whatever. I suggest you two get married on Twitter, have fun on Tango, buy your kids on Amazon, and pay for it all through PayPal. And when you get fed up with this new husband, sell him on EBay.

L.O.L. (lots of love), Daddy[18]

As I shifted my career from that of a clinical psychologist of twenty years, meeting people in my office of safety and confidentiality, I began to engage in more executive and leadership, which is all life coaching, even if you don't name it that. However, when I began full-time coaching in 1996, the profession had grown with the Internet and the collapsing of geographical boundaries with it. Although much coaching still took place in corporate offices, it was not expanding to the solo professional or individual looking for a confidante as a coach who could also assist him or her to have more of the life he or she really wanted. And it was now done via phone calls rather than in-person meetings.

As a professional that had been trained and experienced in observing nuances of communication in person (facial expressions, body language, and emotional cues), I was pleasantly surprised at how connected I felt to my coaching clients on the phone, and they reported the same to me. I began to understand that the phone coaching afforded the opportunity for a different and sometimes greater human connection due to fewer

[18] https://www.linkedin.com/pulse/modern-communication-the-rescue-squad?force NoSplash=true

distractions in a focused conversation and a type of connection that allowed a certain degree of anonymity to be strength. In other words, I could not see my clients, but I could still feel connected in the space of our shared conversational purpose.

Benjamin Zander, director of the Boston Philharmonic state in a keynote speech I heard at a conference, that great music comes from the spaces between the notes, a quote also attributed to Erik Satie and Claude Debussy. A coaching conversation is a focused time for the client to speak and be heard and to explore things they had not previously said to another, to dream out loud, and to get real-time feedback, understanding, and support.

Coaching is not about fixing wounds or hearing about one's past, but it is designed to hear about the present and what did the client want to be different in the future—next week, next year, or further out. Coaching affords an opportunity for the client to share dreams he or she might have given up on, to face past fears or obstacles of belief, and to see if there were a new way to integrate those. So there is a certain degree of connection in coaching that is not always face-to-face, but it is always in real time, strengthened by asynchronous communication between conversations.

People who post things online in social media are doing so in an asynchronous manner, not knowing always who will read and respond, and what is posted stays there forever somewhere in cyberspace.

In a recent Pew Research survey, the following data was reported:

> In the current survey, we wanted to understand the broader context of teens' online lives beyond Facebook and Twitter. A majority of teens report positive experiences online, such as making friends and feeling closer to another person, but some do encounter unwanted content and contact from others.
>
> - 52% of online teens say they have had an experience online that made them feel good about themselves. Among teen social media users, 57% said they had an experience online

that made them feel good, compared with 30% of teen Internet users who do not use social media.

- One in three online teens (33%) say they have had an experience online that made them feel closer to another person. Looking at teen social media users, 37% report having an experience somewhere online that made them feel closer to another person, compared with just 16% of online teens who do not use social media.

One in six online teens say they have been contacted online by someone they did not know in a way that made them feel scared or uncomfortable.

Unwanted contact from strangers is relatively uncommon, but 17% of online teens report some kind of contact that made them feel scared or uncomfortable. Online girls are more than twice as likely as boys to report contact from someone they did not know that made them feel scared or uncomfortable (24% vs. 10%).[19]

This research does show that young people today are savvier and more cautious about what is posted and how naked communication might be. Sometimes party photos get posted that they may delete later, but they can always be found. However, the point of this chapter for youth is that nothing beats real-time, live communication (phone, in-person, or even video chat) about something personal, private, and difficult to share. The purpose of true friends, not as in Facebook friends, is to be able to share, to listen or be heard, and to trust that what is shared will be kept private. Even though some promises will be broken and relationship trust will be hurt, life must go on, and new standards of trust will be developed. We can't go through life having no one to share our fears, shames, dreams, and aspirations with.

---

[19] http://www.pewinternet.org/2013/05/21/teens-social-media-and-privacy

Keep trying. Test the waters before a deep dive, and remember you can always share with a trusted and ethical professional, such as a counselor or life coach.

My longtime friend Dave Ellis states in *Falling Awake: Creating the Life of Your Dreams* that we are to choose our conversations. We need to be conscious of what we say to whom and we need people that support our truthful and transparent communication. Dave says even the news and movies we watch are conversations. Sometimes we need to balance the media meme of violence and negative news with positive and uplifting media. From *Falling Awake*, Dave Ellis writes, "Moment by moment, we get to choose our conversations and community. What's at stake is enormous—everything we say, hear, watch, listen to, read, and see. No choices are more powerful than these."[20]

The Dalai Lama, in the book, A Force for Good: The Dalai Lama's Vision for Our World by Daniel Goleman and Dalai Lama, urges us to watch less news as he believes it is toxic. Choosing your conversations could include watching more positive than negative news with some other outlets of heartwarming and inspiring information. Or turn off the TV and go visit nature.

Ok, now you have learned about various roles and ways to choose when and how and with whom to get naked. The next chapter is the one most challenging to us humans…. Relationships.

---

[20] Dave Ellis, *Falling Awake: Creating the Life of Your Dreams* (Breakthrough Enterprises, Inc., 2000).

## Chapter 7

# Naked Relationships: The Challenge of Authentic Intimacy

"Your task is not to seek for love, but merely to seek and find all the barriers within yourself that you have built against it."

—Rumi

"How much we know and understand ourselves is critically important, but there is something that is even more essential to living a wholehearted life: loving ourselves."

—Brené Brown

Let's face it. Relationships are tough, especially those of marriage or committed partners. We often get out of sync, pulled by duties of job, children, health, wealth, friends, family, and so on. But living alone is not what humans are to experience either. So the challenge becomes ways to be naked emotionally in safe places and to do it before the layers of armor are thick and impenetrable. This even applies in the role of parent or work roles that may not be intimate partners, but they can be important mirrors for our life learning and relationships that can help us evolve in important ways.

In romantic relationships, for sexual intimacy, you eventually have to shed your clothes together and make love. I have often found that phrase curious. We don't make anything. We experience love, connection, and sexual pleasure. As Paul McCartney wrote, "The love you take is equal to the love you make."

But lovers are also naked at other times, depending on their need for privacy when they get into bed together, take showers, or change clothes. Everyone has a different need for privacy. Some don't mind walking from the closet naked to grab a new shirt; yet others want the lights out and wear pajamas to bed. What matters is how emotionally naked you can be with your lover, partner, or spouse. When we take off our clothes from a day at work or a night out to dinner, we feel free from the constraints and constrictions that clothes sometimes cause. And that feeling of comfort while becoming unencumbered by constrictive clothing is the same feeling that can come from being able to speak truthfully and authentically to your partner or another one who listens well, for example, a friend, counselor, coach, and so on.

And let me be clear. This emotional nakedness and authentic communication is not done without clear intentions and safety of circumstances. Just like we don't show up physically naked at all times, we likewise don't reveal ourselves completely emotionally at all times. And yet there must be some times to experience that, or the burden and constriction will grow more uncomfortable.

## A Client's Story of Wounded Trust

A female client shared with me she was holding her husband in check from catching him in an affair ten years ago, expecting him now to be honest and faithful. But she wasn't telling him that she also had an affair ten years ago, and her shadow closet would not be cleaned up until she took her husband off the hook and shared her truth and need to control so he would not leave her. Part of what we do as coaches is to help people clean up unfinished business or pieces of a person's life that he or she is tolerating or leaving as a distraction. These sometimes can become a psychic vampire, sucking the lifeblood from his or her authentic being.

Emotions, I believe, are severely misunderstood in modern culture. Emotions seem to be greatly feared because we believe they are impossible to control. We can control physical nakedness with added clothing for protection, comfort, discreetness, beauty, and style. But emotional nakedness is hidden invisibly.

What does *emotional nakedness* actually mean? Part of the reason our culture used to believe that you should not be naked physically with someone before you are married is because we must first learn to be naked emotionally. Physical nakedness is best in the context of emotional and spiritual connectedness. One of the definitions for the word *naked* is being devoid of concealment or disguise. Intimacy, whether sexual or a deep connection with another friend, colleague, or family member, is where emotional nakedness should reside. We don't want to be emotionally naked without cautious choosing any more than we would be physically naked in an unsafe environment or relationship. Once you have the intimacy of a trusting relationship, there should be no need for a disguise.

As most of us know, however, that is easier said than done. Self-protection is a very human experience; one we never really show any need for training. We often self-protect ourselves by concealing and disguising, and we do this just as much emotionally as we do physically. Here are some reasons we wear disguises that make emotional nakedness difficult:

- **Hurt and pain from past experiences:** Sometimes this pain occurred in childhood. Sometimes it happened in previous relationships or marriages. It may even show up in your current marital relationship because of intentional or unintentional conflict. Our past experiences affect our current relationships in incredible ways. In all areas of life, it is important to face and deal with our past. We will always be trapped and our growth stunted if we are unwilling to look into our past and search for freedom from the hold it has on us.

- **Inability to trust in or depend on our spouse:** Marriage is to be a partnership. Committed partners should really embrace their differences, accentuate their unique strengths, and learn collaboratively how to be a couple. Whenever self-centeredness or self-reliance enters the relationship, it is not as it should be. Most of us have experienced several breakups or relationships that were so loving and then became so contentious and empty. I would say that emotional nakedness probably became nonexistent. In order to let go of the disguise, we must learn to work as a team. We must put the needs of our spouse ahead of our own. The disguise can only be destroyed when we are willing to see that we need to trust and rely on someone other than our self.

- **Fear of coming undone:** We live in a culture that values strength, not weakness; self-reliance, not interdependence; and control rather than the unknown. For all these reasons and more, learning to be emotionally naked in marriage is countercultural. Somewhere the fear that our spouse will reject us because of our junk outweighs the risk. We become comfortable with our disguise, and it stays in place because the fear of humiliation and shame doesn't seem worth the effort. We get by and resign ourselves to thinking this is just the way life is.

Margaret Wheatley says so clearly in *Turning to One Another: Simple Conversations to Restore Hope to the Future,*

> The simplest way to begin finding each other again is to start talking about what we care about. If we could stop ignoring each other, stop engaging in fear-filled gossip, what might we discover? … As the world becomes more complex and fearful, we know we need each other to find our way through the darkness. The yearning for

community is worldwide. What can we do to turn to
one another?[21]

The only hope to experience freedom from these masks is humility. To be emotionally naked requires humility. It requires us to humbly admit we don't have it all together and we don't even have words to describe what we are feeling. We have to admit that facing our past scares us so much that we don't want to go on and we have needs we cannot fill. We must admit we can't live life in a pretty little package all tied up with a bow. We need to come undone. None of these things are possible without practicing emotional nakedness and honest self-disclosure and suspending judgment of self and other so truth and authenticity may come forth. So emotional nakedness is hard, but it is so worth it. Brené Brown says in *Daring Greatly: How the Courage to Be Vulnerable Transforms the Way We Live, Love, Parent, and Lead,* "Vulnerability is the core of all emotions and feelings. To feel is to be vulnerable."[22]

I suggest to my clients that e-motion means energy in motion. Don't ignore what you're feeling. Acknowledge it, embrace it, express it, and move the energy. The love you live is equal to the love you give, both for yourself and others.

I'm reminded of a quote from Jean Paul Sartre's famous play *No Exit.* I loved the depth of this play when I studied it in in high school. The existentialist writers of Sartre, Hegel, Kierkegaard, and Heidegger fascinated me, but this line, "Hell is other people," always caused me to reflect.

That statement always bothered me because I am a people person and I believe other people teach, help, and, of course, challenge us. But can you really call that hell? No way could that be true.

Later on in my psychology courses, I came to believe that the statement reflects a perpetual human dilemma. From an early age, we

---

[21]  Margaret Wheatley, *Turning to One Another: Simple Conversations to Restore Hope to the Future* (Berrett-Koehler Publishers, 2002).

[22]  Brené Brown, *Daring Greatly: How the Courage to Be Vulnerable Transforms the Way We Live, Love, Parent, and Lead* (Avery, 2012).

want to control our world, and from some deep place, other people challenge that daily, and it becomes hellish perhaps for many of us. The simple way to state this is to say, "People, you can't live with them, and you can't live without them. Even a hermit needs a crowd to escape from."

From *Turning to One Another: Simple Conversations to Restore Hope to the Future* by Margaret J. Wheatley, it says,

> Relationships are all there is. Everything in the universe only exists because it is in relationship to everything else. Nothing exists in isolation. We have to stop pretending we are individuals who can go it alone. We humans want to be together. We only isolate ourselves when we're hurt by others, but alone is not our natural state—separating ourselves rather than being together.[23]

Sigmund Freud once said that what is important in life is to love and to work. For many of us, it is easier to work well than love and be loved well. That may be because intimacy is where the greatest struggle often takes place. According to research done using the FIRO-B, a psychometric instrument that determines fundamental interpersonal relations orientation, intimacy is the area for most people with the biggest gap between what they express and what they want. (Sourced from https://en.wikipedia.org/wiki/Fundamental_interpersonal_relations_orientation)

What I mean by love in this chapter is not the usual sense of love as romance or intimacy with a partner. The world's major spiritual teachers agree that there are only two real emotions: love and fear. I speak of love here in the same sense as spiritual leaders and writers. Love, as an emotion, is the absence of fear. Love is a potential we want to experience. Love is a state of being, a love consciousness our clients can access that allows them to be courageous, purposeful, and in harmony with their values.

---

[23] Margaret Wheatley, *Turning to One Another: Simple Conversations to Restore Hope to the Future*, 2002.

Love is experienced in the body as well. When experiencing love, our body feels expansive. We feel centered, grounded, energized, available, and in touch with our whole being, what some might experience as a state of bliss. This state is the opposite of fear. When we experience fear, our body contracts. Physiologically, fear causes our muscles to tighten and prepares us to flee, fight, or freeze. We know from research that states generated by fear literally cause our field of sight to narrow, giving us tunnel vision. We literally experience our world as contracted, more limited, and more threatening. This is why we say love is all you need. When in doubt, come back to love as a centering point.

In common understanding, love is also the act of creation. So when people are attempting to create something new in their lives, love is the state that allows them to be creative. We create the feeling of love through connecting: to people, to the earth, to life itself, or to something larger than ourselves. Whether we realize it or not, we are always connected. Once we are conscious of this connection, love can occur.

One basic issue that is encountered frequently in life coaching is that clients feel isolated, particularly in industrialized cultures like that of the United States. They may feel this as loneliness. I coach them to acknowledge the connectedness they live in. Connectedness is a quality of life for all human beings, and to be unaware of our own connectedness is to be unaware of love.

Because human life is a connected life, the quality of each depends on the quality of our relationships with family, friends, community, a higher power, and us. When one or more of these relationships becomes unfulfilling, our life becomes unfulfilling.

**Expressions of Love**

A great song by the Beatles is the 1967 tune, "All You Need is Love." You may be old enough to have heard it on the airwaves, and of course, the songs of the Beatles are ubiquitous today as well. It was easy to remember, and it carried a profound, timeless message. Written by John

Lennon and Paul McCartney, "All You Need Is Love" repeated the title line over and over throughout the song. It addressed the listener directly as "you," reinforcing the personal message that love is an essential and powerful force for change. This is a message that coaches often use with clients, encouraging them to care for and appreciate others, as well as to let love in. And that, of course, requires vulnerability and trust.

Sometimes love scares us because it can bring hurt. It has said that Mother Teresa tried to make sense of this for a reporter who asked her how to love without being hurt. She said, "I have found the paradox that if I love until it hurts, then there is no hurt, but only more love." A Dr. Martin Luther King Jr. is reported to have echoed her poetic statement of this paradox, "Darkness cannot drive out darkness; only light can do that. Hate cannot drive out hate; only love can do that.

(There is no proof of who said this but a powerful statement nonetheless.)

Sometimes our role as parents requires us to love until it hurts. Especially for parents of adolescents, loving until it hurts seems like a hard road. The *National Longitudinal Study on Adolescent Health* found that a sense of connection at home and school were the two conditions most protective of children's well-being. It was the perception of connection itself that was key, not any specific program or set of actions.

(The National Longitudinal Study on Adolescent Health Preliminary Results: Great Expectations
Jonathan D. Klein, MD, MPH. *JAMA.* 1997;278(10):864-865. doi:10.1001/jama.1997.03550100090045.)

For adults and parents of adolescents alike, Harry Palmer's (author of The Avatar Course) definition of love offers us a hand to hold in times of frustration. "Love is an expression of the willingness to create space in which something is allowed to change." Some people resist intimacy and love because they seem confining, a prison of sorts. Being separate feels somehow safer.

## Learning to Love Ourselves

Most of us are taught early how to love others (that we should love others), but we do not learn how to love ourselves. Many have been taught that to love ourselves is wrong, even a sin. Consequently many clients in midlife discover they do not love themselves very much at all. I believe we need to learn to love ourselves so we have the capacity to fully love others. Think of the metaphor of a cup that, once full, has enough reserve to give to others. If all people do is empty their cup all day—through conflict, stress, and worry—and are not having experiences that refill their cup, they have nothing left to give to others. When they arrive home, they cannot give to spouses, children, or themselves. Be aware of when your cup is empty. Consider what you can do to refill yourself.

Loving ourselves is nothing we need to feel ashamed of or embarrassed about. Loving ourselves actually makes us more loveable. In addition, loving ourselves teaches us how to love and care for others, which means we are able to love others more richly. Sometimes this is the task of coaching, to help clients recover their capacity to love.

Before we can love someone else fully, we must care for ourselves. Before we can fall in love with someone, we must fall in love with ourselves. Loving ourselves will attract people to us. People who love themselves are a delight to be around. If you have ever been around someone who lacks self-love, you know how distressing that can be. Underneath a thin veneer of adaptation to what others expect lies a pool of self-hatred. It depletes us to be around that kind of energy. Those who love themselves naturally love others and have a respect for others and their well-being. Self-love creates positive energy that attracts more positive energy.

Until we truly create a loving relationship with ourselves, other relationships will not be as fulfilling as they could be. When we do not love ourselves, we look for others to fill the void, which drains the energy from our outside relationships. When we love ourselves, we do not have to look outside to have our needs met. Therefore, we can simply enjoy the other relationships for what they are. Outside relationships do not have to compensate for what we are missing inside. They can add to it. This can make the love of others that much sweeter because it is the extra, the icing on the cake.

Self-love is the quiet, inner sense people carry that tells others they are competent, valuable, and worthy of giving and receiving love. Self-love is critical for mental health and happiness, as well as the best insurance against mental distress and depression. A person with self-love can face and handle the shocks and setbacks that inevitably happen in life. Without self-love, the problems of life are more difficult. Something is always missing that can only come from within.

When people lack self-love, they find it difficult to take care of their self. As they learn to love themselves, their willingness and ability to care for themselves increases.

## Love Is a Choice and a Verb

Love is a choice, not simply or always a rational choice, but rather the willingness to be present to others fully without pretense. What does this statement mean to you? You may reflect on the fact that being present—authentically present—makes exquisite sense and sounds simple. Yet it is very difficult for many of us.

If love is a choice, a key question becomes, "What gets in the way of choosing love for you? What do you choose instead of love?" I ask clients to do this as a fieldwork activity, noticing over the course of a week what they choose instead of love or connection. Common examples of what people choose instead of love include self-focus, anger, judgments, expectations, being right or busy, and worries. Once we have identified what gets in the way of choosing love, we can then consider these questions: How did you choose these instead of love? How can you help yourself choose love instead?

Some people can begin a practice of some sort to begin to build their capacity to choose love. One thing we know is that many people who report feeling very fulfilled have practices associated with gratitude. Keeping a journal in which clients record at least three daily statements of gratitude is highly associated with increased joy and lowered incidence of depression.

In my training of thousands of coaches, I have utilized the following to assist in clients embracing the concept of love as a choice.

(I want to acknowledge my longtime friend and colleague Diane Menendez for much of what is adapted here as I learned much of it from her co-writing and co-teaching with me)

## The Compassion Exercise

The exercise is based on and adapted from the writings of Harry Palmer, creator of the Avatar Course, who believed, once people are honest with themselves, they will feel compassion with others. That is, people need to recognize they are not special but are simply human beings, just like other human beings. Those they are angry with are human. With this humility comes compassion for themselves as well as others.

This exercise actively demonstrates the powerful role of mind-set and its impact on the clients' emotions and well-being. The clients pick a specific person on which to focus for the exercise and then complete the following five steps mindfully.

1. With attention on the person, repeat to yourself, "Just like me, this person is seeking some happiness for his or her life."
2. With attention on the person, repeat to yourself, "Just like me, this person is trying to avoid suffering in his or her life."
3. With attention on the person, repeat to yourself, "Just like me, this person has known sadness, loneliness, and despair."
4. With attention on the person, repeat to yourself, "Just like me, this person is seeking to fulfill his or her needs."
5. With attention on the person, repeat to yourself, "Just like me, this person is learning about life."

Many of my colleagues have used this exercise with clients by reading the steps to them as they focus their attention on the person.

Most clients report a shift in their emotions after the exercise, which usually brings them to a sense of compassion for the other person that might have been missing earlier. I also find it brings about the sense of connection that is the foundation for love, as I have been describing.

A coach I know once tried a variation of this exercise with a client who was having difficulty justifying any time she spent on her own self-care. She asked her to identify someone she respected and cared about, whose way of treating herself she admired. She then asked her to visualize herself as that person—acting as if—and to look from that friend's eyes onto her own face, repeating the five steps. This exercise resulted in a great sense of personal peace and opened up the possibility of self-care for this client.

## Expressing Love

Earlier it was stated that human beings learn better how to love others than how to love themselves. Through this exercise, I ask you to learn how you can better love yourself. These exercises are meant to be done with another person, but they can be done alone and use journaling for self-reflection.

1.  Ask, "What do you do for a person you really love? What do you do for or with that person?" Someone might say that he does things he would not do otherwise, such as scratch his wife's back without being asked or pay really close attention and listen when someone talks about her day.

2.  Ask, "Do you do the same for yourself?" For the person above, the response may be, "So you do something your wife loves without being asked. How often do you do things for yourself without others asking you or prompting you to do them?" Or "So you pay exquisite attention, really listening to that person. How often do you pay exquisite attention to yourself, really listening to yourself?" Most people report they do a better job with others than they do with themselves in the specific ways they show love. That leads to the next question.

3. Ask, "How can you do more of this with yourself? How can you pay more exquisite attention to yourself, to really listen to yourself?" This exercises focuses on doing, the actions that spring out of the feeling of love. It is important to identify specific actions in step one in order to get the clients to consider what actions they can create for themselves. As coaches know, actions can shift attitudes.

## Expressing Care

1. Say to yourself (or the person you are doing this with), "Think of something—a concrete thing—that you own and really value and care about. What is it?" Write down the answer. Some examples have included a family photograph album that goes back two generations, a piano, a Mont Blanc pen given to them as a gift, and a 1957 Chevy Corvette.

2. Ask, "How do you take care of it?" Make sure you get specific actions here. The person may put the photograph album in a place close to her, protected from light, to preserve it. She also says it will be the first thing she grabs if there is ever a fire or disaster. She dusts the piano every week, polishes it every other week, keeps its keys covered, and has it tuned regularly. The other person keeps the Mont Blanc pen in a special leather case so other things in her purse will not scratch it. And another keeps the 1957 Chevy Corvette in a garage and does not take it out when the weather is bad. He drives it carefully and has it maintained by the best mechanic he knows. He does not use it for everyday driving, but reserves it for special occasions and celebrations.

3. Ask, "How could you do similar things to take exquisite care of yourself?" Treat this statement as an analogy, and find analogous actions by brainstorming. This can be a stretch—and a lot of fun—for both you and your trusting partner.

a. "So you put the photograph album in a safe place to protect it and preserve it. Are there ways you can better protect and preserve yourself?" This person ended up thinking about the fact that she did nothing really to preserve her skin. She started a skin care regimen.

b. "So you keep your piano very clean, well-covered, and polished, and you tune it regularly. Are there ways you can do those things for yourself?" This person thought the question was a stretch but realized she does not go regularly to her doctor for checkups (that is, "tuning"), needs to take better care of her nails and hands ("covering the keys"), and really loves massages but does not regularly get one ("polishing it").

c. "So you keep the pen in a special leather case so it won't get scratched. Are there ways you need to keep yourself from being hurt needlessly?" This person realized she tended to walk and move so fast that she bumped into things and was always getting scratched or bruised. This led to a discussion about slowing down and paying attention as a way of protecting herself.

d. "So you reserve your car for special occasions, keeping it out of situations that will potentially damage it and keeping its engine maintained. How can you keep yourself out of harm's way and keep your body maintained?" This person decided to have his cholesterol checked and stop taking on a particular kind of consulting gig, one that was stressful and brought him into contact with companies whose cultures were harsh and bruising. He decided he was not reserving himself enough for things that could be celebrations. Work did not have to be so bruising.

*Patrick Williams*

## The Power of Forgiveness

In order to foster healthy self-love, we may need to forgive ourselves, just as healthy love of others requires us letting go of resentments, old angers, and unresolved wounds. Forgiveness can be difficult to give when revenge seems more appropriate. Yet it grows out of love and can change the course of a life.

In a time when many leaders are unable to say they are sorry or offer forgiveness, this story shows the power and wisdom of forgiveness:

> During the American Civil War, a young man named Roswell McIntyre was drafted into the New York Cavalry. The war was not going well. Soldiers were needed so desperately that he was sent into battle with very little training.

> Roswell became frightened—he panicked and ran. He was later court-martialed and subsequently was condemned to be shot for desertion. McIntyre's mother appealed to President Lincoln. She pleaded that he was young and inexperienced, and that he needed a second chance.

> The generals, however, urged the president to enforce discipline. Exceptions, they asserted, would undermine the discipline of an already beleaguered army.

> Lincoln thought and prayed. Then he wrote a famous statement. "I have observed," he said, "that it never does a boy much good to shoot him."

> He then wrote this letter in his own handwriting: "This letter will certify that Roswell McIntyre is to be readmitted into the New York Cavalry. When he

serves out his required enlistment, he will be freed of any charges of desertion."

That faded letter, signed by the president, is on display in the Library of Congress. Beside it there is a note that reads, "This letter was taken from the body of Roswell McIntyre, who died at the battle of Little Five Forks, Virginia."

Given another chance, McIntyre fought until the end. (from Riches of the Heart by Steve Goodier. Life Support System Publishing; 1st edition (December 10, 1999)

When I ask clients to consider this true story, they often realize that Lincoln's forgiveness changed the course of a life. They can consider where forgiveness—for himself or herself or for someone else—might be offered as wisely and generously as Lincoln's. And what a lesson in naked decision-making!

## The Water Bearer, a Teaching Story

A key task of naked loving is learning to love ourselves so we are available to love others and receive love. In the teaching story below, the water bearer learns how love can turn flaws into gifts through acceptance. (This story is found in many cultures, and the source is unknown, but it has been passed down for centuries.)

A water bearer in India had two large pots, which hung on each end of a pole that he carried across his neck. One of the pots had a crack in it, and while the other pot was perfect and always delivered a full portion of water at the end of the long walk from the stream to the master's house, the cracked pot arrived only half full.

For two years this went on daily, with the bearer delivering only one and one half pots of water to his master's house. Of course, the perfect pot was proud of its accomplishments. But the poor, cracked pot was ashamed of its own imperfection and miserable that it was able to accomplish only half of what it had been made to do. After two years of what it perceived to be a bitter failure, it spoke to the water bearer one day by the stream.

"I am ashamed of myself, and I want to apologize to you."

"Why?" asked the water bearer. "What are you ashamed of?"

"I have been able, for these past two years, to deliver only half my load because this crack in my side causes water to leak out all the way back to your master's house. Because of my flaws, you have to do all of this work, and you don't get full value from your efforts," the pot said.

The water bearer felt sorry for the old cracked pot, and in his compassion he said, "As we return to the master's house, I want you to notice the beautiful flowers along the path."

Indeed, as they went up the hill, the old cracked pot took notice of the sun warming the beautiful wildflowers on the side of the path, and this cheered it some. But at the end of the trail, it still felt bad because it had leaked out half its load, and so again the pot apologized to the bearer for its failure.

The bearer said to the pot, "Did you notice that there were flowers only on your side of the path, but not on the other pot's side? That's because I have always known about your flaw, and I took advantage of it. I planted flower seeds on your side of the path, and every day while we walk back from the stream, you've watered them. For two years I have been able to pick these beautiful flowers to decorate my master's table. Without you being just the way you are, he would not have this beauty to grace his house." (Story found here: http://www.sacinandanaswami.com/en/s1a38/wisdom-stories/the-cracked-water-pot.html)

This story is often used with clients to help them recognize that each of us has our own unique flaws. We are all cracked pots. But if we will allow it, our flaws will be used to grace our own and others' tables. In the connected world we live in, nothing goes to waste. We need not be afraid of our imperfections and our flaws. If we acknowledge them, we too can be the cause of beauty. In our weakness we find our strength.

## Reflections on Love and Seeing Anew

Anthony de Mello, a Jesuit priest who grew up in India, brought the benefits of being in the present—of meditative practice—to everything he did. He writes eloquently on the relationship of love and mind-set in one of his most famous books, *Awareness*. He states how we must let go of our need for the approval and love of others in order to truly love. He uses the terms drug and addiction(s) below to refer to our attachment to fitting in, gaining others' approval, and staying busy and distracted.

I encourage you to read *Awareness* because the lessons he describes here often become some part of what clients bring to coaching. They are ready to understand the distinctions between love and need and between love and attachment. This may apply to your path at this moment. He says, for example,

If you wish to love, you must learn to see again. And if you wish to see, you must learn to give up your "drug." It's as simple as that. Give up your dependency … To see at last with a vision that is clear and unclouded by fear or desire. You will know what it means to love. But to come to the land of love, you must pass through the pains of death, for to love persons means to die to the need for persons, and to be utterly alone.[24]

## Reflections on Love: A Client's Story

Marilyn, a participant in a 2001–2002 training of my coach training school, Institute for Life Coach Training, was moved by the class on love. She sent Pat and Diane, the instructors, the following eloquent piece of writing based on her personal experience of losing her husband and her subsequent thoughts about love, loving, and the place of love in coaching. We liked it so well that her writing became an integral part of the ILCT class on the power of love. I print it here with her permission.

Our culture commonly assumes that love is a "something"—almost quantifiable—that is given by one person and received by another. We know, especially from general psychology, that love is essential to a full human life—perhaps even essential to biological survival. We almost believe it can be "poured" from one heart into another heart, like lemonade from a pitcher. We usually think that if a person does not love a child, that child is doomed to experience life as empty of love and therefore be unable to give love to others. With this assumption, we often go through life wishing for more love from others—and we seek it sometimes in very odd places.

---

[24] Anthony de Mello, *Awareness* (Image, 1992).

Yet the seers, sages, and saints of the major spiritual traditions do not understand love in that way. They universally say that love is our own essential nature, pure and lasting. They say that this ultimate love is the core of every human heart, that the only reason we do not experience it all the time is that it is covered up by a mountain (or a thousand veils, or a darkness—the metaphor depends on the tradition) of lesser realities. These include all our self-centered desires and aims, our focus on the senses, and the chatter of the mind.

Love, they say, is constantly available, no matter what is going on around us, no matter how life may seem to be treating us. Love just is—flowing, spontaneous, and independent. Love sustains. Love is divine; it is God. Love is never absent. It's just that we are sometimes unaware of its presence, or we misunderstand the meaning of our experience.

This truth about love has become clear for me in the process of spiritual unfolding. But it became unmistakable soon after my beloved husband died. From that time to this, at the thought of John, love springs up, full and beautiful, in my awareness. His body, his personality, all the qualities that I associated with him is gone from this earth. Early in our marriage I would have said that he loved me, that he taught me to love by giving me his own.

Now I know better: the quality of his presence, his awareness of inner love, evoked my own awareness of Inner Love. That is why it can endure now. It was always there within me—I needed only to come to recognize it and revel in it. It is still true: I need only become aware and it is there for savoring, for resting, for delight unlimited.

Do I forget love? Yes. But not as often or as thoroughly as I used to. Is the love I experience all there is? Hardly! Love is infinite. We are pilgrims in love and pilgrims into love just as truly as we walk through air and let it fill our bodies.

These reflections are not included to demonstrate that the sages are correct in their assertion that love is our true nature and dwells equally in all. They are, rather, meant to stimulate us to ask these huge "what-if" questions:

What if love is our true essence and it is therefore accessible to anyone and everyone? What if love is, in fact, always present within us and therefore always available to our perception?

Here are some thoughts in response to those questions.

- No one would be seen as helpless to discover love because the field of inquiry would not depend on another, but rather on one's own willingness to look deep within.
- Romantic love and spousal love could be reframed as a particular expression of the essential inner love, thereby freeing relationships from thinking such as, "If you loved me, you would ..." and "I want you to love me more."
- We could acknowledge, when we "feel loved" by another, what is really happening is that something in the quality of the other's presence stimulates our awareness of our own inner love. This happens perhaps most easily when the other is aware of her inner love. This awakens us, momentarily at least, to the reality of love in our own center.

- The experience of love is independent of circumstances; it can be accessed even in great pain. It does not require the presence of another human being, although two human beings focused on love bring immense joy to living.
- Doubts about whether one is lovable are also dispelled with the experience of inner love. In fact, the question disappears. There is love, flowing and grand, within oneself. The experience dissolves even the question of whether I am lovable. Instead, I begin to understand that I am love.

In the modern world, definitions of love are common narratives in magazines, blogs, and pop culture. Our difficulty seems to be that English is not the best language for expressing nuances of profound subjects. It is, however, the language that many of us use. Translations to another language add an additional challenge, but love is expressed in all languages and cultures.

I use the Greek words (*Eros, agape,* and *philia*) to try to define various types of love. We easily say what love is not, for instance, what we feel about our car. Some say that love and sexual involvement are equivalent, while others disagree. I suggest a reframing to think of love as the force or capacity that is the source of all our feelings of wonder, gratitude, beauty, affection, concern, interest, enjoyment, and fondness. As the endless capacity that makes all these experiences possible, it may well be beyond definition. Perhaps that is good!

Our society seems to believe we have confused ourselves about love so much so that Kevin Cashman, in *Leadership from the Inside Out: Becoming a Leader for Life,* says it's a forbidden word in business circles.[25] It seems true that we are confused, but perhaps we have only mixed in other inner states with love and are not making the necessary distinctions. We have mixed love with attachment, for example, so we may feel we "love her/him/it so much" that we must have him/her/it in our lives to be happy. We as a society have mixed love with sex so that

---

[25] Kevin Cashman, *Leadership from the Inside Out: Becoming a Leader for Life* (Berrett-Koehler Publishers, 1998).

many cannot tell the difference between the two. Akin to this is the confusion between love and infatuation.

If love is the capacity flowing beneath all our positive experiences, creating our delight in the beautiful, lovely, and the precious, love is always present within us, revealing to our perception its many-faceted nature in infinite ways, all of them quite grand. You can call it Inner Love.

I share here a story told by Rachel Naomi Remen in her 2000 book *My Grandfather's Blessings: Stories of Strength, Refuge, and Belongings.* When she was a child, her grandfather described to her eight levels of giving and their relative worth. She promised to always "do it right," meaning to give in the highest way. Her grandfather's reply was, "Some things have so much goodness in them that they are worth doing any way that you can."[26]

Love is like that, so utterly good that all expressions of love, no matter how mixed or how confused they may be, are worth including in life. If we know this, then to touch a flower tenderly, to experience a romance, to revel in a new possession, and to dedicate oneself to the Divine may all have similar value because they all spring from that deeply inward capacity called *love*, that capacity which is our true nature.

As long as we imagine love to be a something given and received, we also feel that love is limited, it is dependent on other people, and it can even be destroyed or come to an end. Again the seers and spiritual writers disagree with this. They insist that love is infinite, strong, steady, constant, dynamic, and always accessible. It does not end. It does not depend on other people or circumstances. They say that all we need to do to uncover this immense love within ourselves is to focus deep within our being.

If all this is true, what are the implications for authentic living?

- All of us should be practitioners of some form of entering within. The most common one is meditation, which itself has a number

---

[26] Rachel Naomi Remen, *My Grandfather's Blessings: Stories of Strength, Refuge, and Belonging* (Riverhead Books, 2001).

of forms. Just spending quiet time with a focus on the physical space of the heart can open the awareness to the great inner love. (See below for more on this.)

- If a person is aware of her own inner love while she works with a client or relates to a loved one, the other person will also experience his own inner love, creating a wonderful atmosphere in which relating can occur more lovingly with insight and great joy for both the loved and the lover.

- Once we are in touch with inner love, it can be directed toward people, work, visions, and goals or the Divine, anywhere we choose to direct it.

- Even if someone you love is not aware of this loving energy in which he or she is surrounded, there will be a shift and an opening in the relationship. It cannot be otherwise since awareness of our own inner love is the most creative force that exists.

## An Experiment to Consider

There are many ways of becoming aware of inner love. You may already know and practice methods that keep you aware of love. You also may want to experiment with the following:

- Take a few minutes to still your mind and body. Focus on your chest in the area of your heart. Just hold your attention there until your mind slows down a bit. Be aware of inner movement. Watch. Love can arise as a subtle thread or a full-flowing river. Let it be. Once you notice it, let your attention rest there and watch it increase in power. Enjoy it for as long as you can.

- Sit comfortably and take a few deep breaths. Recall an experience during which you felt great love or a person for whom you felt great love. Allow yourself to get in touch with that situation again as fully as you can. Now ever so gently, shift your attention to the love you felt, and let the object of your love or the trigger for the experience fade from your awareness. Focus on the love alone. There it is, in your own heart. Stay with it as long as you wish. Return gently when you are ready.

- Again, while relaxed and quiet, simply request inside to experience the love that is there. Wait. It will appear.
- Practice acting as if love is the root of your being, your anchor, and your constant nourishment from within and is always accessible. While doing this, you may wish to pause often to check in with your own heart.

Once we have practiced becoming aware of our own inner love and have discovered that it is not so hard to access whenever we are willing to be attentive, we can direct this experience of love wherever we want. If we are with our favorite person, we can become aware of love inside and then direct it to him or her. If we are coaching, the client becomes our direction. If we are dealing with a difficult person, we can direct inner love to him or her. The possibilities are as infinite as love is infinite.

A former client, who as a young entrepreneur began some naked truth conversations about his dad, wrote about it in his book.

Today I forgave my dad.

I haven't talked with him in over 10 years. But today after a four-hour drive I said, "Hi Dad".

I walked up, we shook hands and I said:

"I forgive you."

"I'm sorry." And

"I'm putting the past away."

The past is behind me now. I'm letting go. That doesn't mean I want to cultivate a relationship. That doesn't mean I have anything more to say right now.

Before, during and after all this my heart raced a bit. I had to remind myself to take appropriate breaths.

But it feels good to feel.

It feels good to breathe.

I'd say that was the hardest thing I've done or the scariest thing I've done, but I've given myself a lot of practice letting go lately. And over the past few years I've done a lot of things that take me to my edge in fun, adventurous, and even uncomfortable situations.

If I'm going to live the things I talk about and write about and go as deep as I'm about to go on the project I'm working on right now, I have to take massive action. I have to follow though and commit. I needed this more than he needed my words.

Forgiveness isn't always for the other person. The anger and pain of not forgiving is like holding a hot coal— you're the one getting burned.

Forgiveness can be hard. But you can begin to forgive without even talking to the other person. With practice you can forgive the guy who cuts you off on the freeway. You can forgive the person who talks behind your back. Who doesn't follow through? Who can't keep their word?

As you begin to live with higher virtues yourself, you'll be tested. You'll have to forgive. Accept. Care. You can forgive me for posting this on Facebook even if you

didn't want to see it. You can forgive yourself. Let go!
Forgive. Love.[27]

Engaged living is courageous living. We are all so very imperfect, and
the act of forgiving, to me, is one of the highest levels of compassion.
By doing this you allow the energy to flow in an area that needs your
love and attention as well. Sometimes we don't want to look at those
areas, or we need more time to consider what to do with them; however,
once the time is right, we take the step and release those ties that have
bound us. We release ourselves from the story we've woven over time,
and then we are truly free. When we give attention to and take action
on (the harder of the two) the areas in our lives that we sometimes don't
know what to do with, we uncover how we really are.

One of my favorite passages from one of my favorite books, Hugh
Prather's **Notes to Myself**, includes:

> If I had only … forgotten future greatness and looked at
> the green things and the natural world and reached out
> to those around me and smelled the air and ignored the
> forms and the self-styled obligations and heard the rain
> on the roof and put my arms around my wife … and
> it's not too late.

And he continues,

> Relationships with the world, with people we meet
> are also an important part of a full human experience.
> What do we learn from others view of us, or our
> perceived interpretation? If you walk down a street and
> see someone waiting for a bus, or you sit across someone
> on the subway or in some waiting room, do you notice
> you look and make contact or do you look away?

---

[27] Jimmy Tomczak, *Lakeside & Tide: Inspiration for Living Your Best Life Now* (Wet
Star Press, 2016).

Are you avoiding looking a stranger in the eyes because you don't want to make them uncomfortable, or do you turn your eyes so they cannot look into you?

What is there in you, that you don't want them to see?

Hugh Prather ends his beautiful book this way,

> Being real is more a process of letting go than it is the effort of becoming. I don't really have to become me, although at times it feels that way—I am already me. And that is both the easiest and the hardest thing for me to realize.[28]

## The Effect of Alcohol Abuse on Relationships

I have one final thought on the challenges of getting naked and being transparent and authentic in relationships. An elephant in the room that is often ignored in relationship breakdowns is the abuse or overuse of alcohol or other substances to excess. How does alcohol abuse affect communication in marriage or other intimate relationships? I include it here as important and available information.

- *Damaging communication.* With alcoholism and marriage, alcoholic spouses tend to use more negative and damaging communication (e.g., criticizing, blaming, contempt), express more anger, and show lower levels of warmth when trying to solve a problem than do nonalcoholic spouses. This kind of negative communication discourages the use of positive problem solving skills such as open discussion and encouragement.
- *Less problem solving.* Couples in which one partner is alcoholic engage in problem solving less often than do other couples. Partners in such marriages may lose the desire to engage in

---

[28] Hugh Prather, *Notes to Myself: My Struggle to Become a Person* (Bantam, 1970).

problem solving and give up when alcohol is involved because they anticipate that the conversation will soon become negative. As this pattern continues with alcoholism and marriage, important issues such as family finances, sexual intimacy, and childrearing decisions go unresolved because it is easier to avoid communicating than it is to deal with the stress and negative emotions that are associated with alcohol-related communication problems.

- *Personality characteristics.* Personality characteristics common among alcoholics also can affect communication. Alcoholics tend to be less conscientious, less agreeable, and more anxious and hypersensitive than are nondrinkers. These personality characteristics make effective communication and problem solving more difficult.
- *Effects on the brain.* Researchers believe that alcohol's effect on the brain may contribute to the increase in the negative communication. Alcohol appears to impair a person's ability to understand and properly interpret what a spouse is saying. Alcoholics tend to interpret things their partners say in a very negative way and this leads them to respond with greater anger and negative emotions. Is alcohol abuse related to violence in marriage? Alcohol abuse is frequently related to marital violence:
- Among battered women, 40–60 percent reported that their husbands were heavy or problem drinkers. Among married men admitted to alcohol treatment centers, 50–70 percent reported participating in partner violence, with 20–30 percent of these men reporting having engaged in severe violence towards their spouses.
- The more frequently men are intoxicated, the more likely they are to be verbally and physically violent toward their spouses. Alcohol abuse is connected to increased aggression and marital violence that tends to be more severe and more likely to result in injury.
- Spouses under the influence of alcohol tend to act more aggressively, perhaps because their ability to think rationally is

reduced. Alcohol tends to make individuals more impulsive and to decrease their ability to restrain their aggression. This pattern is especially noticeable among spouses who are more aggressive even without alcohol.[29]

For the concept of getting naked emotionally to be effected especially in intimate, loving relationships, it is important to know that excessive alcohol abuse (or other drugs) will most likely lead to the opposite kind of communication. In fact, the excess drinking or drugging may be to cover up and keep buried some sharing that would be part of healing and achieving more wholehearted living if not under the influence of substances.

From relationships to self. We sometimes lose our self in the WE.... the next chapter will highlight challenges and important insights in self-awareness and your body.

---

[29] http://www.learn-about-alcoholism.com/alcoholism-and-marriage.html

# Chapter 8

## Skinny Dipping: Being Comfortable in Your Own Skin

"The moment will arrive when you are comfortable with who you are, and what you are—bald or old or fat or poor, successful or struggling-when you don't feel the need to apologize for anything or to deny anything. To be comfortable in your own skin is the beginning of strength."

—Charles B. Handy

Can you remember the first time you were aware of being naked? Perhaps as a young child or more likely as an adult while skinny dipping in some hot spring in the wilderness, visiting a Japanese spa, or running naked on the beach on a secluded island. (Okay, I admit to all those, but how about you?) Or maybe it was the first time you made love and felt so naked and free or naked, embarrassed, and uncomfortable. Hopefully that changed over time and with experience. Perhaps for some, this experience of being naked was not so freeing. The vulnerability was not safe or experienced in a positive manner.

These are some of the people for whom this book is written, the walking wounded, the *scarred*, and the *scared* who may not show that secret part on the outside, but it lives within them. This book is also about those who may not be scarred nor have deep hurts, but instead have unrealized dreams or something in them that wants to be called forth. If those parts are never shared, they are likely never to manifest. This may include relationships, workplace, community, neighbors, and professional organizations, anywhere there may be an opportunity to share authentically. Your greatness may be waiting to be manifested, if you share it with another, in naked truth.

Once we are naked in a safe and secure place, we feel free (if we are comfortable with it), and we reveal ourselves with all of our warts and wrinkles to those we are with. Maybe you have only been naked with a lover or spouse; perhaps you have had the experience of clothes-optional hot tub or hot springs in an idyllic setting with strangers you will never see again. So you revealed yourself briefly to more than one other familiar person, but so did they! And how many of you have been to Sweden or Finland where, after dinner, the whole family invites you into their sauna sans clothing! To them that is tradition and nothing to be embarrassed about!

I do not write this book to recommend unbridled nudity. This is about being naked metaphorically, yet to most, that feels equally scary or provocative. This book is about finding places, spaces, and people where you can be naked metaphorically, emotionally and soulfully. It's where you can reveal yourself in full spectrum humanness.

I am not proposing that you be overly transparent and vulnerable everywhere, but you can be smart and protective of these special places and relationships where you can be comfortable in your own skin and let yourself be naked in safety. We often use phases like "naked truth," "baring your soul," or similar phrases that indicate an atypical expression of emotions or a personal story unshared that lies under the surface.

Of course we need to be clothed and protected from weather and abuse and covered for comfort and safety. The same is true for emotional nakedness. Pick and choose carefully the places to be revealing. You only need a few special people and places. Some might use a therapist, life coach, spiritual director, minister, or best friend, but the real opportunity comes from nurturing a few relationships with those you love and trust most where you can be real.

With the feeling of being naked and shedding the protective armor, we must experience responsibility, safety, and trust. We need to trust and be responsible for our own safety and protection, and we need those around us at those moments to be trustworthy and protective. If not, then find new places and new people.

> Being comfortable in your own skin means to be satisfied with yourself. Often, in American culture, and certainly for women, this is interpreted in terms of appearance. However, true satisfaction and self esteem reflect your ability to cope with whatever challenges life has for you.[30]

My premise in this book is that we can never live fully or optimally if we have no places where we can be naked. As a psychologist I often helped people complete "unfinished business" (from Gestalt theory and Fritz Perls) and find the safety of my office and confidential space as a place to share what they had not shared elsewhere.

That itself can be freeing, but then the goal was to assist them to find safe spaces and relationships outside in the real world where they could be totally revealing when they needed or wanted to or when they needed to be truthful about a deep feeling or old hurts, trauma, grief, and loss.

As a life and wellness coach, I am more inclined to give people a sacred space in our conversations to reveal those parts of themselves that are unfulfilled, unrevealed, unrealized, and often unspoken outside of their own psyche.

---

[30] Read more at http://www.ehow.com/how_2292328_be-comfortable-ones-own-skin.html.

## Rediscovering the Uniqueness of the Body

Several centuries after he said it, the philosopher René Descartes's statement, "I think, therefore I am," is still the predominant paradigm, at least in the United States. We live in a disembodied world, so to speak, where the body is reduced to a vehicle or platform for our heads instead of our hearts (aside from times of usefulness like giving birth). Or the body is objectified, conveyed as a sexual object or an object of shame, as when someone experiences his or her body as too heavy, too lean, too skinny, too short, too tall, or too something. We have become gifted at denying the body as a vehicle for living, knowing, and learning. Many people treat their bodies as if they are machines—not "me" but "it." The term *somatic coaching*, commonly used to describe focus on the body and emotions in coaching, is based on the original Greek word *somatikos*, which means the wholeness and inclusiveness of the living, aware, and fully embodied person.

Pablo Casals, the famous cellist, wrote in his book *Joys and Sorrows*,,

> Each second we live is a new and unique moment of the universe, a moment that will never be again … And what do we teach our children? We teach them that two and two make four, and that Paris is the capital of France. When will we also teach them what they are? We should say to each of them: Do you know what you are? You are a marvel. You are unique. In all the years that have passed, there has never been another child like you. Your legs, your arms, your clever fingers, and the way you move. You may become a Shakespeare, a Michelangelo, or a Beethoven. You have the capacity for anything. Yes, you are a marvel. And when you grow up, can you then harm another who is, like you, a marvel? You must work—we must all work—to make the world worthy of its children.

Casals calls attention to one of the great losses of our age, that is, our learning institutions treat children as if logical thinking is what counts for living. Although our capacity for thinking may be what makes human beings distinct from other members of the animal kingdom, it does not naturally or inevitably create the kind of fulfillment in living that is the birthright of being human. I extend Casals's thought to my clients as marvels, complete with minds, emotions, bodies, and spirits deeply interconnected.

Life and wellness coaches take a holistic view of coaching, seeing the client's fulfillment in living his or her life optimally as the context for the coaching. While many clients come to me prizing their intellect and rationality over their emotional, physical, and spiritual resources, their journey to full humanity may invite them to reach beyond this realm. In reality, my clients' language, cognition, emotions, body, and spiritual selves are interconnected. I view each of these as pathways, or doorways, you might enter and invite exploration of your self-fulfillment.

## Living an Embodied Life

Many coaching clients experience themselves as "having my body" as opposed to what is more real, that is, "I am my body." Consequently, when they experience stress, become frightened, or go through a difficult period of transition, they neglect the resources available to them through noticing what they feel bodily, exploring their sensations, centering, and discovering available resources regarding the nonhabitual ways they use and carry their bodies.

A basic principle of embodied living is that all of us have habitual ways of responding to life, and these include habitual ways that we hold our bodies, breathe, and move. I have learned in my various experiences with body work, that how you move through space is how you move through life. Just noticing how you move through space offers a vehicle for both noticing and changing how we move in our lives. Do you move quickly—walk fast with your head forward, talk fast, breathe fast, and hold your chest high? Do you move more slowly—speak clearly with intentional pauses and fill the space these pauses occupy with a calm energy?

I believe that our bodies are tremendously underutilized resources for learning and change in life. When we speak of intuition, we are really acknowledging the wisdom of the body.

> Intuition can be seen as how the middle prefrontal cortex gives us access to the wisdom of the body. This region received information from throughout the interior of the body, including the viscera—such as our heart and our intestines—and uses this input to give us a "heartfelt sense" or what to do or a "gut feeling" about the right choice. (Siegel. (2011) *Mindsight: The New Science of Transformation* Random House)

When you cultivate the ability to observe whatever you are experiencing without judgment, simply noticing, you begin to gain more present awareness. In coaching, I ask clients to notice body sensations, emotions, thoughts, impulses to action, interior dialogue, memories, sounds, and images and to simply witness them without judgment.

An underpinning of this work is the Gestalt point of view around contact, an essential function of the healthy human is to be able to use one's energy to connect with self and others in a healthy way. Effective contact with one's self or another means there is a meeting place where an exchange occurs and creates the possibility of change and growth. You can see this when two people greet each other and make eye contact in a comfortable way, acknowledging each other and connecting in an exchange of energy. Through connection and an exchange, something new may be created for each of the elements whose boundaries have come into contact. When I observe someone who does not meet the eyes of someone he or she is speaking to, I see someone who is maintaining a very tight personal boundary, limiting the intensity of the exchange by deflecting contact. The principle I work with is to foster increased sensory awareness so my capacity to be aware and in contact with self will enable me to be available for fuller contact with others.

Margaret Wheatley so beautifully writes in *Turning to One Another*, "Relationships are all there is. Everything in the universe only exists because it is in relationship to everything else. Nothing exists in isolation. We have to stop pretending we are individuals that can go it alone."[31]

## Our Aging Body

Learning to become comfortable in your own skin may start with just you, but eventually it has to include someone else. Once we are in relationship with a significant other, we have learned to project the persona we think we are or pretend to be rather than to just be the person we are. Society and the fashion and diet industries give us a message of wearing our clothes better or losing weight and getting in better shape. And that's not all bad. I love that I can still play tennis four days a week and remain in good health, but I certainly don't look or feel like I did in my twenties, thirties, forties, or fifties. But I can't do anything to get younger. I can only take the best care possible of me now, and I will never look like the bodies that are in advertisements for fashion or food.

In 2016, there were two reality television shows that were both not only comical but sometimes insightful. The show *Naked and Afraid* has a man and a woman, both of whom have some survival and wilderness skills, to meet each other naked in a challenging remote environment, and they are expected to work and live together with no water, food, and clothes for twenty-one days. Very few have made it to the end for the $25,000 prize.

And another show that is even stranger is *Dating Naked*, an American reality series. The show, focused on a man and a woman, attempts to create a match between two participants who are completely naked. The man and woman first go on a date with each other. Then they have two additional dates with other people, all in the buff. I don't

---

[31] Margaret Wheatley, *Turning to One Another: Simple Conversations to Restore Hope to the Future*.

recommend that level of transparency in learning to be authentic, but to each his own!

How do you look when you look in a mirror? What are your feelings about your looks? Your skin? Your wrinkles or spots? I am all for skin care and sunscreen, and I love massage and pedicures, but my body still is not how I would like it to be.

Here is the harsh truth we forget to remember. From the moment you came into this world, you have been steadily progressing toward death. Ouch! I realize that doesn't sound good. But from the moment you took your first breath, it became inevitable that, at some future point, you would take your last. The question is: what have you done in between? And what can you do now as if you are still part of vital aging and not mediocre living?

No matter your age as you read this book, if you are not in the last one-third of your life, you will still have had experience around those who are elders. Both my wife's mother and my own mother passed away from cancer in a hospice facility. And those experiences at the end of life were very enlightening to me. Knowing that someone is near death and witnessing the gentle and peaceful approach of a hospice is actually spiritually uplifting. I was at my mother's bedside often over a relatively quick slide from diagnosis to death, and I was there at the end to touch her face and say good-bye.

As a person approaches the very end of life, two types of changes occur. Physical changes take place as the body begins to shut down its regular functions. And there are changes on the emotional and spiritual level as well, in which the dying person lets go of the body and the material world.

In some ways the process of dying is like the process of being born. Over nine months, a child goes through many stages of development that lead at last to labor and birth. In a similar way, a person with advanced illness goes through many changes over an extended period of time with a set of clear changes occurring in the final stage. I was at my mother's bedside as she passed, having just flown in from out of state. Over the many weeks I was at her side previous to this ensuing finality, the last few days were an amazing though sad experience. Her skin had become soft and smooth like that of a newborn, and as I stroked it and said good-bye and how much I loved her, I know she was unconscious, but I still believe that her spirit or higher consciousness knew I was there and touching her soft skin so gently.

The good thing about getting older is that you can be more accepting of the changes in your body and have an attitude of "Who cares?" The perception of older people who in most cultures and looked upon as the wise elders are not supposed to be the young and the beautiful. By the time you are in the last decades of your life (which varies by culture), your relationship with your body is to do the best you can to stay vital and active, but you also get to not care so much about what people think. Aches and pains are accepted if they have to be, but aging gracefully is the goal, one that is not easily achieved.

You may find the next exercise helpful.

### The Dis-identification Exercise to Connect with the Self behind All Identification and Attachment

The following is extracted from *Psychosynthesis: The Elements and Beyond* by Will Parfitt (used with permission). Roberto Assagioli, founder of Psychosynthesis, said "We are dominated by everything with which our self becomes identified. We can dominate and control everything from which we dis-identify ourselves."

The following exercise is a tool for moving toward and realizing the consciousness of the self. This procedure, called the "self-identification" or "disidentification" exercise, is of vital importance and should be done with the greatest care. If you feel at all tired, do not read on from here until you have at least taken a break. You will enjoy this exercise more if you are fresh when you first try it out.

1. Relax yourself in the best way you know how, putting yourself in a comfortable but alert position. Take a few deep breaths, and let go of any tensions from the day. Follow the instructions slowly and carefully. Affirm to yourself the following, "I have

a body, but I am not my body. My body may find itself in different conditions of health or sickness. It may be rested or tired, but that has nothing to do with my self, my real I. I value my body as my precious instrument of experience and action in the world, but it is only an instrument. I treat it well, and I seek to keep it in good health, but it is not my self. I have a body, but I am not my body." Close your eyes, recall what this affirmation says, and then focus your attention on the central concept, "I have a body, but I am not my body."

2. Attempt to realize this as an experienced fact in your consciousness. Now affirm to yourself, "I have feelings, but I am not my feelings. My feelings and emotions are diversified, changing, and sometimes contradictory. They may swing from love to hatred, from calm to anger, and from joy to sorrow, and yet my essence—my true nature—does not change. I remain. Though a wave of anger may temporarily submerge me, I know, in time, it will pass; therefore, I am not this anger. Since I can observe and understand my feelings and can gradually learn to direct, utilize, and integrate them harmoniously, it is clear that they are not my self. I have feelings, but I am not my feelings." Close your eyes, recall what this affirmation says, and then focus your attention on the central concept, "I have feelings, but I am not my feelings."

3. Attempt to realize this as an experienced fact in your consciousness. Now affirm to yourself, "I have a mind, but I am not my mind. My mind is a valuable tool of discovery and expression, but it is not the essence of my being. Its contents are constantly changing as it embraces new ideas, knowledge, and experience and makes new connections. Sometimes my thoughts seem to be independent of me, and if I try to control them, they seem to refuse to obey me. Therefore, my thoughts cannot be me, my self. My mind is an organ of knowledge in regard to both the outer and inner worlds, but it is not my self. I have a mind, but I am not my mind." Close your eyes, recall what this affirmation says, and then focus your attention on the central concept, "I have a mind, but I am not my mind."

4. Attempt to realize this as an experienced fact in your consciousness.

Next comes the phase of identification.

5. Affirm clearly and slowly to yourself, "After this disidentification of my self, the I from my body, my feelings, and my mind, I recognize and affirm that I am a center of pure self-consciousness. I am a center of will and capable of observing, directing, and using all my psychological processes and my physical body." Focus your attention on the central realization, "I am a center of pure self-consciousness and will." Realize this as an experienced fact in your awareness.

Once you have practiced this exercise a few times, you can use it in a much shorter form. The important point is to keep to the four main, central affirmations:

- I have a body and sensations, but I am not my body and sensations.
- I have feelings and emotions, but I am not my feelings and emotions.
- I have a mind and thoughts, but I am not my mind and thoughts.
- I am I, a center of pure self-consciousness and will.

Some people find it difficult to follow the affirmations in this exercise that say you have but are not your body, feelings, or mind, objecting that this may cause a disassociation from these functions. A suggested alternative way of using the exercise, if this bothers you, is to change the disidentifying statements to "I have a body and sensations, and I am more than my body. I have feelings, and I am more than my feelings and emotions. I have a mind and thoughts, and I am more than my mind and thoughts." This is almost as effective, but the original as designed by Assagioli uses the principle of affirmation through negation, which can have a particularly powerful effect on creating the required conditions for self-identification.

You may have to repeat the exercise a few times to start with to get its full flavor, but then you will be able to do it daily from memory. The effort will be well worth it. All the influences that try to capture your attention and demand identification will no longer have the same hold over you.

## The Bare Essentials: Looking Inside for Answers

The following is a personal story of naked vulnerability and courage from a friend and colleague who, after being an active outdoors person for many years, became a paraplegic from an illness with sudden onset.

> Thoughts looking out the hospital window about 3 weeks after the spinal cord stroke:
>
> *I had always thought of myself as "a strong, independent woman". As a paraplegic, I asked myself "Now who are you, Patricia (not her real name) ... now who are you"?*
>
> *As I was enduring the undignified experience of a nurse assisting me with bowel and bladder function, I was faced with encountering myself as a new person ... I wondered who I would be or become. I soon realized that this experience required more courage, grace and strength than any experience in my life.*
>
> *I didn't need to redefine myself. But I did reframe my self-definition to fit the new context of my life.*
>
> *Over time, I realized that I am indeed still a strong, independent woman, but also a woman who is more aware of my weaknesses and limitations as well as my need to learn how to accept and ask for help.*

————

*People asked me if I got depressed—maybe surprisingly, I did not. I believed that I did not have the luxury for depression. (I felt like I would be too good at it ... meaning I could sink into tears and remorse, do nothing constructive to rebuild my persona and life, and perhaps never feel whole again.)*

———

*I had to keep what's familiar and within my control, which for me was my work, because I had little control over most of my body. My professional life felt like something I could figure out and that I knew how to navigate. So work became a comfortable place to focus my attention and time, and gave me a sense of strength and power while I was adjusting to this life change and gaining a newfound sense of my physical self.*

*As it happens—I realized early on that I had never, ever been as proud of myself as I am now.*

———

*My mantra became "Be patient with yourself" and to remember that I did everything I could do.*

———

*People will not or cannot always show up for us the way we hope ... so we have to show up for ourselves. When we are courageous enough to reveal our thoughts and feelings, it means we are also taking the risk of not getting what we need or want from the other. I learned to become more OK with that in that I gained a fuller acceptance of myself that was not dependent on the perceptions of others.*

———

*Opening up to others:*

*I realized the importance of sharing information about my disability with those who had "a need to know". While I shared openly with a few of my friends and family, in most cases what they seemed to hear was filtered by their needs and priorities. It was necessary and right, in my opinion, to inform some people I worked with/for so they would understand if I had limitations that influenced my work. Thankfully, I was in a career with people who know how to listen constructively and my work relationships opened the door for me beginning to reveal more about my experiences and how they impacted my life. Over time a few of these people became some of my best advocates and supporters.*

*Most times I just want to talk and share the experience of trust and acceptance with another – I may not even need a response. I think that is probably true of most of us – More importantly, we want to be heard and to know our life is being witnessed.*

———

*"All you have to do is."*

*When hearing this, it always causes me to raise my eyebrows ("here goes" I think). There all always two to three times more steps for me than for most people to accomplish something that requires physical movement. Simple things have become complicated, i.e., changing a light bulb or getting my mail requires calling someone to help, coordinating their availability around my work schedule, and other challenges just accomplish a simple task.*

*"I know"*

*I don't expect you to know … I don't even want you to know, I hope you never "know". And I've come to understand that it would be unfair for me to expect others to "know". Paraplegia changed how I had to navigate life on so many levels, making the simplest things complex. There is no way another person can "know" if they don't have a shared experience of it. The speaker may never feel heard on a felt-sense level, if we only respond I know consistently.*

*However, when talking and explaining something to my best and oldest friend Julie, she nearly always responds with "I know". That is a perfunctory, unthinking, meaningless response—no better than when we say, "I'm fine" when folks ask how we are. After 14 years of hearing "I know", I finally realized that I should have told her years ago that the "I know" response left me feeling empty and not heard. It's as if the listener isn't taking in what is being said or absorbing my words with any depth of thought.*

*Better to hear—Thank you for sharing that, I hear how hard that must be, or I hear how that must affect you, or how can I help?*

*Conversation Partners—A Mutual responsibility*

*I plan to have a courageous conversation with Julie very soon because it has caused a real rift in our relationship that needs to be bridged. I didn't accept my side of the responsibility for being a good conversation partner by not trusting enough to disclose the effect this was having on us, our relationship. Now I need to have the courage to self-disclose and reveal how I'd like our conversations to be going forward.*

*If we expect others to listen to our "reveal", then we have the obligation to not conceal how their responses impact us or are perceived by us.*

*Hugs: The Mother-load. The best response is a Hug … it says more than words and is universal*

———

*Quote I like from Rod McKuen … Hippie, popular poet of 1960s and 1970s.*

*"I don't apologize for being hard to know … but apple pie and warm hands help" (from Listen to the Warm)*

As you turn the pages now to the final chapter, you'll find it is also a beginning…. a beginning of your journey to more freedom and authentic living. Enjoy!

# Chapter 9

# Prison Break: You Had the Keys All Along

"Everything can be taken from a man but one thing: the last of human freedoms - to choose one's attitude in any given set of circumstances, to choose one's own way."

—Viktor Frankl

"Life is not a problem to be solved, but a reality to be experienced."

—Soren Kierkegaard

We arrive in this world naked, and we will leave this world naked. Yet we won't remember either experience. But now there is a new choice for the interim, naked living. My invitation is to experience more emotional transparency, which empowers readers to celebrate the dare of nakedness within carefully conceived boundaries. This teaching memoir has shared with readers not only the profound benefits of getting naked (emotionally and wholeheartedly), but also several ways to determine when, where, and with whom you can be naked emotionally and spiritually. After all, for the grand leap of self-exposure, it makes sense to start with a safety net.

We have spent most of our lives clothed, protected from weather, society's norms, and our own learned embarrassment. Do you remember as a kid loving to be naked, or have you witnessed young children and their gleeful nudity? My daughters as toddlers and their children as toddlers threw off their clothes in an exuberant expression of a freedom that proudly declared a moment unencumbered.

This book is not about physical nakedness. It's about being emotionally naked and transparent, being spiritually vulnerable, and having the willingness to expose one's deepest truth. I define naked living as the ability to be vulnerable, honest, transparent, shame-free, and unburdened. This requires the presence of a confidante, friend, coach, or counselor as the witness to your authenticity. Getting naked takes the metaphoric view of nakedness as an emotional and spiritual value in our human growth and development. Emotions, in our culture, are greatly feared because we believe they are impossible to control. While we can modulate our physical nakedness by adding clothing, emotional nakedness is more challenging to monitor.

Intimacy is ultimately about nakedness. We don't want to be emotionally naked without careful discrimination any more than we would want to be physically naked in an unsafe environment or relationship. Self-protection is a very human instinct, one at which we are universally proficient. Yet when you can be intimate with a trusted other, there is no need for a disguise.

One of the most important reasons I wrote this book is because I am fascinated by how we become more whole by finding ways to be naked emotionally with trusted people in safe places. Becoming whole implies becoming more of who you are meant to be, more unapologetically yourself. And becoming whole is inextricably twined with being fully seen by another. There has to be a witness. You can be physically naked by yourself, but being emotionally naked alone serves no purpose, no true revealing. It must be a relational experience with a trusted other.

## Breaking Out of Your Self-imposed Prison

You have created your own prison from time to time in life. You may have things you are afraid to share that may be shaming, hurtful, or just plain uncomfortable. But you also have some beautiful and unique desires that you may have kept under lock and key.

You've already read how important and necessary is to have a safe place to be when needed, but that does not have to feel like prison. You will learn in this chapter how to express any unshared parts of your life and how to experience living on purpose when it leads to emotional freedom and a more fulfilling and complete human experience.

I believe that my profession of personal coaching arose in the latter part of the twentieth century and is flourishing today for two main reasons:

1. Humans have a lack of connection to others and purpose. Many of us have acquaintances and friends, but we don't really feel connected to meaning and purpose.
2. There is a shortage of listening. We need people in our life that can really hear us, both what we need to say and to evoke from us what we are not saying, and to speak it out loud to a committed listener.

Each of us looks for fulfillment and authentic happiness in our own way. According to Carl Jung, life purpose and spiritual searching most often emerges in midlife after we have experienced a variety of life's ages and stages.

Sometimes the yearning for fulfillment becomes a call so loud and intense that we cannot help but step off the path we are on and devote ourselves to the search for fulfillment. As many midlife seekers discover, fulfillment often means returning to deep sources of satisfaction that we may have had glimpses of many years ago. At that earlier time, we may have lacked the courage to follow the call, or we may have allowed life's stresses and serious pursuits to cover up the glimmer of what we knew to be true.

This pattern takes place in the lives of so many because each of us has a life purpose that, we believe, has been with us since we were very young. At moments when we experienced a profound sense of being in the flow—being in the right place at the right time while using our gifts—we are likely to be living out our life purpose. Life purpose calls us forth. It may be a calling we answer, something larger than our small selves that deeply connects us with others with what is larger than ourselves. I have noticed that discovering one's life purpose often begins with a sense of experiencing a calling, a compelling vision or sense of some more meaningful way to be present in your one unique life.

Bookstores are filled with information about our contemporary search for meaning. We know that life purpose has become an important focus for many. Rick Warren's 2002 book, *The Purpose-Driven Life*, has become the best-selling self-help book of all time. A common definition of life purpose is a calling, an overall theme for your life or intent that transcends daily activities. A quick search indicates that the word *purpose* means many different things to different writers. A variety of spiritual leaders and traditions say the ultimate purpose of our lives is to remember who we are and to whom we owe our lives and to feel joy.

A rich purpose statement should, in fact, be big and inclusive enough to compel the clients to expand. As Marianne Williamson said so eloquently in *Return to Love*, "Your playing small does not serve the world." A good purpose statement creates the energy to play large. A purpose statement is a private thing, unlike a company's vision statement that hangs on the wall. It is something we use privately to create our goals and life. No one but you ever needs to know your life purpose unless you choose to share it with others.

However, finding a trusting friend, group, or personal coach can really be a way to shine the facets of this diamond you have protected. It will become a working life purpose and guide you in all you do in relationships and what you say yes and no to.

Your purpose is not necessarily something you suddenly discover midlife. In fact, it has probably been with you for quite some time, though you may never have articulated it. This is why you will benefit from revisiting your past and working with some real experiences of being on purpose.

When we are on purpose, we live from our being, our core self. When we have lost track and are living off purpose, our life feels less fulfilling. Many people discover, once they have chosen work or a way of life that is not fulfilling, it is because they have lost sight of their purpose. They have become a human doing instead of a human being.

## Using Life Purpose as a Compass

Almost all persons benefit from life purpose work if they have adequate willingness and a capacity for self-reflection. Some need to be taught the value of reflection in order to benefit from life purpose work. Working with a life coach or spiritual director, you will experience powerful questions that guide your focused attention and lead to introspection. This can be helpful in developing the ability to self-reflect, as can meditation practices, journaling, and many of the other tools available to you.

Some clients come to me with a strong need to reexamine life purpose. They may seem to have lost their way. If they were a boat, we would say they lacked a rudder and were adrift in a sea of circumstances. Some people may feel as if they are surviving but only with a struggle, or they may be striving to achieve but do not feel much satisfaction in their accomplishments.

Sometimes in the natural cycle of life, clues emerge that suggest life purpose work may be called for:

- A client in midlife feels listless, fatigued, and disenchanted.
- The client has experienced losses—deaths, unemployment, or health issues—that make the old way of living no longer possible.
- The client is overwhelmed with life and asks, "Is this the life I really want to lead?"

- The client has undergone significant life transitions—children have left, retirement is near, divorce has occurred, and so on.
- The client feels a serious mismatch between current work and/ or roles and the deep desires of the self.

Remember that life purpose work can be very therapeutic. It can be done using a coach approach either by you or by referring you to a coach who specializes in life purpose coaching. And there are many books and online resources for getting clear on your life purpose.

## Life Purpose Work and Deep Change

In our private as well as professional lives, getting back on purpose may require some startling changes. Living from a deep place is not easy to maintain in twenty-first-century life in the United States, where speed, multitasking, and constant noise make lack of depth a fact of life. Living from a deep place may require you to undergo deep change. As Robert E. Quinn, the organizational behavior and human resource management expert and consultant, wrote,

> Ultimately, deep change ... is a spiritual process. Loss of alignment occurs when, for whatever reason, we begin to pursue the wrong end. This process begins innocently enough. In pursuing some justifiable end, we make a trade-off of some kind. We know it is wrong, but we rationalize our choice. We use the end to justify the means. As time passes, something inside us starts to wither. We are forced to live at the cognitive level, the rational, goal-seeking level. We lose our vitality and begin to work from sheer discipline. Our energy is not naturally replenished, and we experience no joy in what we do. We are experiencing slow death ... We must recognize the lies we have been telling ourselves. We must acknowledge our own weakness, greed,

insensitivity and lack of vision and courage. If we do so, we begin to understand the clear need for a course correction, and we slowly begin to reinvent our self.[32]

The truth is that almost any moment offers us an opportunity to live out our life purpose. By choosing work, relationships, avocations, creative pursuits, and other life elements consciously, we can find the most fulfilling ways to experience our purpose. Life purpose work also helps you to begin to sense and live out a higher level of consciousness.

Consider the following example: What level of consciousness do these people seem to be exhibiting? Is there a transitional stage, an urge toward transformation of consciousness at work in their lives? How might life purpose work be of assistance?

## An Example of Life Purpose Work

Consider the case of Derrick, a thirty-eight-year-old coaching client, who is a teacher and workshop leader. Derrick is happily married with two children, and he is considering whether or not to start his own business. He has been a high school teacher and counselor during his entire career and says he finds himself "sort of itching to make a big change in my work."

## Derrick's Life Experiences of Being On Purpose

Derrick shared the following as times in his life when he felt connected and living his purpose:

- Staying with my grandmother for two months after her husband of sixty-three years died unexpectedly
- Being the only child in a blue-collar family to graduate from college

---

[32] Robert E. Quinn, *Deep Change: Discovering the Leader Within* (Jossey-Bass, 1996), 78.

- Being there for the birth of my two sons
- Adopting two babies from China
- Committing to completing a master's degree in counseling to enrich my work as a high school counselor
- Working successfully as a counselor at the high school
- Creating a special support group program for young unmarried fathers at the high school
- Moving in to care for my father, a widower, for the six months before he died

## Derrick's Life Purpose Themes

Imagine you were a committed listener for Derrick, and he shared his naked truth for the future he wants to create. As Derrick shares the experiences with you, you note the following words and phrases recurring time and time again throughout his stories. These become his purpose themes:

- Connecting to self, others, and the whole
- Fun and different every day
- Friends and connections
- Peace
- Creativity
- Challenges
- Persistence
- Learning
- Believing in myself and my capabilities
- Coming into my own
- In the right place doing the right thing
- Committed, conscious, and courageous

## A Life Purpose Statement for Derrick

The life purpose statement Derrick drafted after this work was the following:

> My life purpose is to create connection between myself, my clients, and all those I contact to the universal whole of life through joyfully living and transforming our life challenges into sources of creativity and learning.

## Using Life Purpose as a Guide

The real benefit of knowing one's life purpose comes when you use it as a guide to make choices and decisions that lead to greater, more authentic happiness and fulfillment. Life purpose work leads you to discover new choices, as well as become clear about directions to pursue and choices to release.

Helping professionals regularly encounter clients who have been living out roles, values, and commitments that were assigned to them early on by their family of origin. Clients often seek coaching because those old ways no longer work. Once they discover their individual life purpose, they may discover, with sadness or with elation, that the roles they have chosen to play and the line of work they pursued have never fit them well. This discovery often leads to a realization that they feel called to live out a different purpose, one that is uniquely their own and may have nothing to do with their family's desires or agenda.

This happened to a client who had spent twenty years working as a divorce lawyer, never feeling a sense of fulfillment from the work. When he did the life purpose work, he chose only one of his twenty-five on purpose examples from his legal career. Most of the examples he chose came from his church work, his volunteer work as a Big Brother, and his ten years of service to the board of education in his township. Recognizing what these choices meant to him about his fulfillment at work, he felt deeply sad and needed to do some grief work before moving forward with his life work. He gave himself time for grieving, and then he was able to articulate his life purpose in this way: "Through intuitively catalyzing people and ideas, I create understanding, awareness, and connections that enhance people's lives."

Imagine he asks you this question, "Is there any way I could live out my life purpose in my work as an attorney?" What changes might he consider that would create a better fit between his purpose and current professional role?

Choosing the title of this chapter, *Prison Break*, was an ironic choice as I have done professional coach training with federal prisoners in which they believe they have turned their lives around, whether still incarcerated or when they returned to society and made better choices, living a life they had not even dreamed of. One of my professional coaching books, *Becoming a Professional Life Coach*, was used in a federal penitentiary as the textbook for a forty-hour coach training course. This is the same curriculum that is taught to graduate degree professionals who come to the Institute for Life Coach Training to become certified professional coaches.

The dozens of men who have been trained in this prison (many of whom have completed an advanced course) now utilize peer-to-peer coaching in the facility, and the warden, psychologist, education director, and chaplain have told me how different they see the men behaving with each other, their family on visitations, and other men who have not had any of the coach training.

Another female prisoner utilized the coach training in her institution to get a job with the mayor's office in a major city as a community services specialist with the Office of Returning Citizens. In other words, she has learned to use her life coaching skills with men and women reentering society after time behind bars. She had discovered her true purpose after eighteen years in prison herself!

So what do you know about your own prison? How have you kept yourself from feeling free? What do you really want to be doing? Where do you really want to be living? With whom would you like to be more honest? What's missing in your life that you would like to experience or pursue?

Don't get me wrong. Not all desires can come to fruition without hard choices. If you suddenly sell all possessions and go on a life purpose quest, you may hurt people in your lives. But how can you begin to come out of your prison that you find yourself in at times and express your deepest longings? Who could you share that with and begin to explore what living on purpose would mean?

In *The Secret* and many other titles by life champions such as my colleagues, the late Wayne Dyer, Cheryl Richardson, and others, we learn, "If we believe it, we'll see it." Or if we begin to live as if what we want in the future is real now, the future may actually occur in seemingly magical ways.

I have done work on life purpose for years, both for myself and my clients. I have found it enlightening if, instead of asking "What do you want for your life?" we ask instead, "What does life want for you?"

Hugh Prather, in *Notes to Myself: My Struggle to Become a Person*, writes,

> Today never hands me the same thing twice and I believe that for most everyone else life is also a mixture of unsolved problems, ambiguous victories and vague defeats—with very few moments of clear peace. My struggle with today is worthwhile, but it is a struggle nonetheless and one I will never finish.

We are always in a state of becoming, but if we keep ourselves imprisoned and protected always, we will become what we already are and live as we already do … and nothing else.

Further on in *Notes to Myself: My Struggle to Become a Person* is my favorite passage.

> Perfectionism is slow death. If everything were to turn out just like I would want it to, or just like I would plan for it to, then I would never experience anything new; my life

would be an endless repetition of stale successes. When I make a mistake I experience something unexpected.[33]

Every experience is a good experience eventually. We experience both chosen and unchosen change. But even if we experience what we would not have chosen, we eventually have to make it a choice and accept what it is and learn from it so we can move from what was to what will be.

And sharing these times in real conversation with a trusted listener is what naked living is really about. Live purposefully, never perfectly.

## Strategies for Living an Extraordinary Life

1. Have a target, a personal mission statement, a life purpose, a compelling future that draws you toward your desired future. You can only prefer your future, not demand it. Planning and goal setting help, but remember that even airplanes are off target 90 percent of the flight. Lots of mini adjustments are made to what is occurring in the now.
2. Have an uncluttered life. This includes physical and emotional clutter. Do a clean sweep of unwanted things, and then work on where and with whom you can be emotionally naked. Work on life's incompletions. It is said that we all come with baggage. A true friend is one that will help you unpack!
3. Live in the present. Sure, you have to envision and think about your future, but it is really unknown and made up. Even your story about the past is just your story.

It has been said, "The past is history, the future but a mystery. The present is a gift. That is why it's called the present."

---

[33] Hugh Prather, *Notes to Myself: My Struggle to Become a Person.*

**Skills to Learn**

1. **Create a toleration-free zone**. If there are things that are bugging you, what I call "gnats and nuisances," things you are frustrated by, then follow the guide of "do it, dump it, or delegate it (or delay it)." By choosing to not tolerate energy drainers, you can take an action of doing something to take care of the toleration. Or you can just dump it. That is, forget it about it, especially if there is nothing you can do. Get it off your list of tolerations. Why waste energy on it? Or you can delegate the challenge. Hire someone who can fix it, or complete a task for you or take it off your radar. Or delay it. Deal with it later, but don't worry about it today. The key here is not to deny it and forget to do one of the other strategies. Just give it time and revisit.

2. **Give yourself extreme self-care.** Be good to yourself. Not just nice but extreme. Reward yourself with something that gives you energy rather than drains you of energy. Get a foot massage. Go to the beach, the woods, the mountains, or lake. Go out for a special treat. Do this periodically, and you build up reserves!

3. **Understand the myth of work/life balance.** (See story below.) Have a center point to come back to. Balance is temporary, but a practice of daily centering and coming back to balance is a very good practice.

4. **Say no and yes with conviction.** When I coach with my clients on living their best life, we get to clarify their purpose early on. Then when they have requests from others or demands of the job, they can consider the request of their time and energy, if it fits with their purpose statements and values, say yes. If it does not, say no. Or at least they can say, "Maybe. Let me think about it." Many people do not tell the truth when others ask them to commit to something or help another, and that lack of naked communication costs them dearly.

5. **Choose to under promise and over deliver.** This is a hallmark of the coaching profession and that of personal or

business development. It does not mean to make promises or commitments that are not well-conceived or important. But it does allow one to have some leeway. For example, if at work, you are asked when you can have a proposal on your supervisor's desk. State you can have it in a week, and deliver in five days. Do this instead of promising something you can't deliver and in a way that will not be polished and ready for review. I'm sure you can think of many areas in personal or family life where this same strategy can be helpful.

6. **Respond vs. react.** This is tantamount to living less stressful and on purpose. As humans we have a natural, built-in reaction of fight-or-flight. But our evolution also allows us to pause for a brief moment and survey the options that may be available to choose instead of a knee-jerk reaction immediately. Even first responders and emergency professionals are trained to react with responses available. They quickly ascertain choices based on their training instead of a less trained person reacting with fear, paralysis, inaction, or unhelpful action.

In summary, to design a preferred personal future, have a plan, and yet be present to life's natural flow. Our life is shaped by incompletions, fears, attachments, addictions, unmet needs, procrastinations, and tolerations. Like barnacles on the hull of a boat, we must have an annual cleaning, at minimum, for smoother sailing.

Clean up your clutter, unfinished business, and incompletions or wounds. Orient your life around your values and gifts. Be an observer of life. Be curious and learn what you are having the opportunity to learn. Life is moving forward always, but you cannot step in the same river twice.

## Story of Cirque de Soleil and Balance

Being a leadership coach for more than twenty-five years, an author of many books, and a teacher of coaching skills, I often discuss the topic of work-life balance for clients. I even suggest the use of a life balance wheel or coaching mandala (see figure below), showing the user the main categories of his or her life, personal and business, and to score his or her level of satisfaction with each. However, unlike some other writers who speak to making the wheel round somehow and getting the same high number in each category, I teach that it is a relative level of satisfaction and may change with circumstances. So it is a measure of energy, focus, and satisfaction, not a static attempt to get high scores and then achieve balance.

**Life Balance Wheel**
**(Coaching Mandala)**

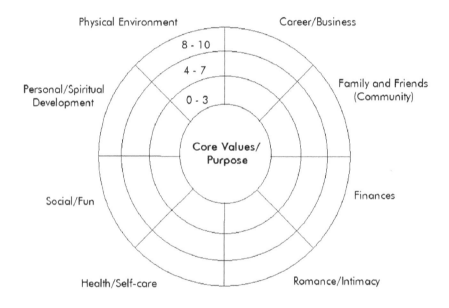

The hub represents your core values—each area interrelated in an ideal life. Give yourself a score (1-10) and shade or color in the space accordingly. Use this Coaching Mandala as a way to assess the level of life satisfaction in each area. You may score it numerically to measure the improvement desired, or you may use it to have a coaching conversation about gaps between where you are now and where you would like to be. Revisit and rescore every 6 months.

Figure 2. Life Balance Wheel.

This was made perfectly clear to me several years ago when my wife and I attended a traveling circus tent performance of Cirque de Soleil in Denver, Colorado. This particular show uses horses and lots of jumping onto horses, trading riders while standing on the horse, twirling objects, and the typical avant-garde characters of a Cirque performance. I was so mesmerized, thinking to myself, "How do they do that? What tremendous balance."

At intermission, when they hope you will buy shirts, programs, and products, I spoke to one of the performers, who was standing on stilts but selling to me.

As he looked down, I stated, "I am so impressed with the balance of you and your fellow performers. Just amazing. I am a life coach, and I try multiple ways to encourage my clients to achieve balance in their life."

To which he replied in his French Canadian accent, "Obviously, monsieur, you were not paying attention. We only achieve balance momentarily. We are in a constant state of motion!"

Wow! The insight that came to me at that moment was palatable. I think I paused in my head, and I was so excited with what I had just learned. I left there thinking that is really what I have believed all these years but was not able to articulate it so well. Our clients (or we) can strive for balance in our activities, the things we are choosing, and unchosen change, but we do it by having a place of balance, or a center, to come back to, a moment in time amidst the competing energies that draw us off center.

I believe it is important to have a daily centering activity such as meditation, walks in nature, yoga, Tai Chi, or even reading. And it is also important to have an instant center to go to in our body when we are thrown off balance in our lives. Additionally, that is why people take vacations away from the routine and the usual. So balance comes from a constant state of motion, as the Cirque character taught me. And our goal for our clients and us is to be purposeful in finding our center, our place of momentary balance that we can take with us and also return to.

What are the key things you do in your life to achieve balance and to center yourself in the midst of competing energies? How can you use this in your life and work?

**Steps to Create a Place of Balance and Personal Power**

1. Think of the most beautiful place you have ever been. Go there in your imagination, and pay attention to all details of sound, visual, and emotional feelings in that place. Then go there in your mind whenever you need to be energized or calmed. This is your place of power, security, and centering.
2. Create a centering routine that you can do effortlessly, for example, a daily walk in nature, bicycling, Tai Chi, yoga, inspirational reading and journaling, or meditating. What else can you choose to have available to you to do routinely?
3. Complete this wheel of life exercise every few months. Check in with yourself on your various levels of satisfaction and not where you might need to give greater attention and action.
4. Take time for self for extreme self-care, quiet, and self-reflection.
5. Embrace and welcome change. It is what it is, and change is constant.
6. Believe in serendipity. Things do happen for a reason, but we don't always know the reason until we figure it out.

We want a compelling future, one where we live freer. Break free of your self-imposed prison. What is your vision? What is your passion? For a life of flow and peace, look forward to surprises, side trips, unexpected experiences, and embracing (not fearing) change.

The present is about learning how the future can be allowed to unfold.

**Ingredients That Help**

- A completed past
- An energized and purposeful present
- A compelling, magnetic future that pulls us forward by irresistible attraction

## Reflections

- "There are no failures ... only results." Thomas Edison
- "We cannot change the direction of the winds ... but we can adjust our sails." Author unknown
- "Insanity is doing the same thing over and over and expecting different results." Author unknown
- "Today never hands me the same thing twice and I believe that for most everyone else life is also a mixture of unsolved problems, ambiguous victories and vague defeats—with very few moments of clear peace. My struggle with today is worthwhile, but it is a struggle nonetheless and one I will never finish." Hugh Prather, *Notes to Myself: My Struggle to Become a Person.*

We are always in a state of becoming, but if we keep ourselves imprisoned and protected always, we will become what we already are and live as we already do ... and nothing else.

I hope you find ways to find the places, people, and moments when you can get a little naked and reclaim your full humanity. And finally, here are some steps to consider for finding a committed listener for deep sharing you know you need to do.

1. Test the waters slowly. You really cannot trust everyone, but you can trust some. And a few is all you need. Educate those who you think you can trust to be confidential. They don't have to fix you. They just need to hear you.

2. Write about your shames, blames, scars, or unshared dreams and aspirations first to yourself. This will help you desensitize yourself to the story you tell. Then have a live conversation about some aspect of this journaling with a trusted other. Do not write details to another at this stage. Share in the moment to hear yourself and to be heard by another who can hold what you share and keep it sacred to you.

3. Hire a professional to speak to, for example, a therapist, counselor, coach, or minister. But research him or her first!

Make sure of his or her credentials and reputation from other clients.

4. Imagine the space in your heart and soul that you will open if that which you have hidden in the darkness is brought into the light. Who will you become? How will you live?

5. Claim your place at the fire. A metaphoric phrase my longtime friend Richard Leider uses to describe finding our *tribe*. Who can be in conversation with as a support group, mentoring, or just for fun and true friendship.

Remember to not take it personally. Opinions are just that. They are not the truth but someone's perspective, just as your view is. The ability and wiliness to stay present to another's nakedness is something that many people cannot do. That is why taking it slow and being cautious but not paralyzed is important. Find your trustworthy few, and cherish them. And you can return the favor by being a committed listener to others.

# Epilogue

Life is continuously providing us information or messages. When we do not listen, the messages become lessons. When we do not learn, the lessons become problems. When we don't address the problems, they become crises. When crises go unresolved, they create chaos in our lives.

Great students of life seek to live on the levels of messages and lessons, not waiting for them to become problems, crises, and chaos. Keeping life's processes on the lesson and message level makes living so much more enjoyable. As is often said, no matter how hard we plan, shit happens. It's what we do with it and how we respond that matters most. Having someone to share your naked truth with is crucial to your resilience. Being witnessed makes you feel held, which in turn makes you more receptive to life's bigger purpose. From there, you can become more capable to reawaken your awareness of your own inner identity, to discover your personal/professional vision and purpose, and to sharpen communication with yourself and others. The ultimate result is being able to live in such an intentional manner that who you are as a person becomes the catalyst for a fulfilling experience of this precious time on earth.

Self-protection is a very human instinct, one at which we are universally proficient. We have all learned to wear masks and protective armor from a young age and rightfully so. The world is not a place to be vulnerable all the time. Self-control defends us against intimacy, letting us track the parameters in order to avoid being absorbed into the spaciousness that resides within.

But if we never let down our guard or take off the masks and the armor, we can never feel the loss of control where true intimacy resides. What is it like to allow yourself to shed your masks and robes and reveal our undefended heart? It is to enter the sacred space of one's own spirit, the *sanctum sanctorum* of the soul. Emotional nakedness can be beneficial alone when journaling or reflecting, but to be truly transformative, you must be reveal your heart and soul to another.

# About the Author

**Dr. Patrick Williams, Ed. D.,**

**Master Certified Coach, Board Certified Coach**

One of the early pioneers of coaching, Pat is often called the ambassador of life coaching. Pat has been a licensed psychologist since 1980 and began executive coaching in 1990 with Hewlett Packard, IBM, Kodak and other companies along the front range of Colorado.

Most recently Pat has focused his coaching on private corporations and Federal government entities going through transitions and adaptive leadership challenges in the nonprofit community.

He is a member of PHI BETA KAPPA and CUM LAUDE graduate of Kansas University in 1972. He completed his masters in Humanistic Psychology in 1975 (University of West Georgia) and doctorate in Transpersonal Psychology in 1977, (University of Northern Colorado) His dissertation was ***Transpersonal Psychology and the Evolution of Consciousness.***

Pat joined Coach U in 1996, closed his 16-year therapy practice six months later and became a full time coach. Pat was a senior trainer with Coach U from 1997-1998. He then started his own coach training school, the Institute for Life Coach Training (ILCT) which specializes in training those with a human services orientation. ILCT has trained thousands of human service professionals on six continents.

Pat is department chair of the Coaching Psychology program at the International University of Professional Studies, and has taught graduate coaching classes at Colorado State University and Denver University, Fielding University, Loyola University, City University of London and many others. He was also a curriculum consultant for the Coaching Certificate program at Fielding International University.

Pat is a past board member of the International Coach Federation (ICF), and co-chaired the ICF regulatory committee. He is past president of ACTO, the Association of Coach Training Organizations and an honorary VP of the International Society of Coaching Psychology. Pat was also honored in 2008 as the educator of the year for the New England Educational Institute.

In May of 2006 Pat was awarded the first Global Visionary Fellowship by the Foundation of Coaching for his Coaching the Global Village, initiative to bring coaching methodologies to villages in developing countries and to leaders of nonprofits and nongovernmental organizations who serve them. He is passionate about coaching and dedicated to ensuring it remains a respected profession.

*Current projects have included teaching coaching to dozens of federal prisoners, speaking at their graduation ceremonies and currently working on a documentary film about the power of the coach approach for those in prison and for re-entry success back into society.*

*And he is a certified trainer for Points of You ™ an international training company with tools for inspiration and creative communication.*

Pat has authored multiple articles and has co-authored the following books:

- Therapist as Life Coach: Transforming Your Practice (2nd Edition 2007)
- Total Life Coaching: 50+ Life Lessons, Skills, and Techniques to Enhance your Practice and Your Life (2005)
- The Law and Ethics in Coaching: How to Solve and Avoid Difficult Problems in Your Practice (2006)
- Becoming a Professional Life Coach: Lessons from the Institute for Life Coach Training (2nd ed. 2015)

Most recently he is a contributor to The Philosophy and Practice of Coaching (Chapter 1, 2008)

Pat continues to coach, train, speak, and lead in the ever evolving field of professional, life, and wellness coaching.

This new book, for a more general public is his first teaching memoir. *Getting Naked: Emotional Transparency at the Right Time, the Right Place, and with the Right Person.*